Kickin' Bass

*Make the Bass of
Your Dreams a Reality*

**By
Robert U. Montgomery**

Praise for Kickin' Bass
Make the Bass of Your Dreams a Reality

"In today's fishing world, having an edge is important. This book will give you that. You'll keep coming back to it time and time again. *Kickin' Bass* will absolutely up your fishing game."
—Rick Hart, *Rick Hart's TightLines, Trophy Smallmouth Fishing*

"Robert Montgomery's book covers all the angles from basic bass biology, bass behavior, locating bass, and the how-to details that help anglers catch 'em to how to take care of fish and our aquatic resources so that anglers can enjoy quality bass fishing for years to come."
—Gene Gilliland, *B.A.S.S. National Conservation Director*

"*Kickin' Bass* is the encyclopedia of bass fishing. From A to Z, Robert's book shares everything anglers need to know to hone their skills to excel at this beloved sport."
—Judy Tipton, *New Pro Products, fish care expert and inventor of V-T2 livewell ventilation system*

"No need to read between the lines. Montgomery hooks anglers with coast to coast expert fishing advice."
—Steve Chaconas, *National Bass Guide Service*

"Once you start reading Kickin Bass, you won't want to put it down."
—Mike Bucca, *Spot Country Bass Guide Service*

"*Kickin' Bass* is a great resource for all avid bass fishermen/women! What a great read!"
—Dale Stroschein, *Wacky Walleye Guide Service*

Also by Robert Montgomery

Better Bass Fishing

Revenge of the Wolf

Love Letters to the Women in My Life

Fish, Frogs, and Fireflies: Growing Up With Nature

Why We Fish: Reel Wisdom from Real Fishermen

Under the Bed: Tales from an Innocent Childhood

Pippa's Journey: Tail Wagging Tales of Rescue Dogs

Introduction

The black bass is easily the most popular game fish in America. For a fisherman, especially a freshwater fisherman, nothing beats a 10-pound largemouth. It's a fish in a million and the fish of a lifetime, and every detail of the epic battle required to subdue it remains etched on your brain in holographic detail for the rest of your life.

What is it that attracts us to bass in the first place and propels us down the lifelong road toward pursuit of a double-digit?

No other sport fish is so available. Although it isn't native to all of them, the largemouth bass now lives in 49 of the 50 states. Only Alaska waters are bass-free. The fact that it has been stocked so abundantly is testament to its popularity.

Also, the largemouth is the most adaptable of game fish. It's not as tolerant of oxygen-poor waters as bullhead or carp, but can thrive in most conditions from shallow lakes and deep reservoirs to turbid rivers and icy streams. It prefers to live as an ambush predator, hiding around cover such as trees, vegetation, and rocks or structure such as humps, points, and ledges. But it can transition to being an open-water hunter when situations dictate.

And this big-mouthed member of the sunfish family is cooperative. Depending on its mood, it will strike just about anything dropped in front of its face. One day as I walked along a lakeshore just before a thunderstorm, I watched bass prowling the shallows. They seemed especially edgy. I tossed a couple of twigs into the water and they struck them aggressively, as if they were the most realistic topwater baits ever created.

This pugnacious nature means kids and even the most inexperienced adults occasionally catch bass by dangling worms for whatever is willing to bite. Looking for greater challenge and excitement, many people become hooked on fishing and gradually replace live bait with artificials. And which sport fish is more available in more waters and more willing to strike than any other?

That's right: Micropterus salmonides, the largemouth bass.

I am blessed to be both an avid bass fisherman and a writer. Assignments for B.A.S.S. Publications have taken me to many of the best bass fisheries in North America and enabled me to fish with and interview some of the best pros, guides, and fisheries biologists. In fact, much of this book's content, in one form or another, was published in *B.A.S.S. Times* from 2009 to 2018. I'm grateful to Dave Precht, vice president of Publications and Communications, for giving me permission to include it.

But I've also added original content—insights you'll find nowhere else—from me and from experts. For example, Captain Steve Chaconas, a Potomac River guide, explains how to catch bass in tidal waters. Captain Dale Stroschein provides tips and strategies for catching smallmouth bass in the Great Lakes. Rick Hart reveals how to boat big prespawn smallies from the tailwaters of dams on the Tennessee River. And veteran angler Pat Helsley outlines how to catch giant bass in those unique fisheries of southern California.

Other contributors include Judy Tipton and Barb Elliott, both experts on how to better care for bass after you catch them. Tipton is the inventor of the V-T2 livewell ventilation system and founder of New Pro Products. As Conservation Director of the New York B.A.S.S. Nation, Elliott has made it her mission to educate anglers about barotrauma and how to treat it so that fish live to fight another day.

Finally, I've included a chapter in each section that begins with "What I Learned . . ." I hope you'll find those insights entertaining and helpful.

I won't absolutely promise you'll catch more and bigger bass if you read *Kickin' Bass*. But the bass is everyman's fish, the world-record bass is everyman's dream, and the information in this book is bound to help if you apply what you learn.

That's the bottom line. A 10-pound trophy fish is a realistic dream for anyone who fishes for bass, and you could be just a cast away from a world record.

PART ONE: Strategies and Techniques

The author thinking like a bass

1. No Rod and Reel Needed

Thousands, perhaps millions, of people have watched the video of an Alabama farmer catching a 16.03-pound bass by hand. Few know the rest of the story.

First and foremost, Robert Earl Woodard's capture of a largemouth just a half-pound off the state record wasn't a one-time stunt. This catch was the culmination of nearly 40 years of practice. If the retired physical education teacher and football coach isn't the only fisherman catching bass this way, he is certainly one of the more experienced.

And the knowledge he gained about bass behavior during those decades can be as valuable to rod-and-reel anglers as any shared by the best pro fishermen and fisheries scientists.

"First of all, bass have different personalities," said Woodard, who has studied the fish, as well as cattle, all his life and writes about being a hard-working farm boy and outdoorsman during a simpler time in a book titled *The Way It was Back Then*.

Lying on his belly at the pier on his five-acre lake, he learned to recognize fish by their individual differences and, as a consequence, gave them names. For example, the 16-pounder is Kickin' Bass (coincidental to title of this book). She earned that label by the way she flips her tail and slaps the water with ferocity after taking a bait.

"But she's also very cautious," Woodard said. "She will suck the bait out of your hand without making contact."

On the other hand, Dynamite explodes out of the water to take a bait, while Jaws, another double-digit lunker, "will bite your thumb and make it bleed," the Alabama native said. Jaws has been caught three times.

Then, there's Bullet, who will knock the shiner or brim out of Woodard's hand, and Sneaky, a smaller male who hides under the pier and waits for just the right moment to steal an offering before a larger female can grab it. Other bass, meanwhile, are more anti-social, and consequently go unnamed.

"We think some never come to the pier," he said. "I saw one with a white spot on top of her tail. And after she went off bed, she went straight back to her territory."

And not only are the bass at Woodard's pier unique individuals, they seem able to tell the difference among people. "I can feed them, but others can't," said the farmer, who pats on the dock as a way of telling the bass that dinner is being served. "Maybe it's the way I present the bait in the water," he added.

"And they feed better when I'm by myself and quiet. They stay back when other people are with me."

Plus, he noted, this observation made him realize that "whenever you can see them, they can see you."

Their above-water-water vision also allows them to distinguish the difference between baits, Woodard added, and an experiment confirmed for him that "matching the hatch" is often important.

"The pond is full of brim (bluegill), so that's what I was feeding them," he said, adding that he decided to spice up the menu with shiners.

"I put the brim in my left hand, the shiner in my right, and threw them out," the retired coach said. "Nine times out of 10, the bass would take the brim, and they seemed to make the decision while the bait was in mid-air."

Now, he's offered shiners enough that the bass also will accept them—when they're feeding. Sometimes they go two or three days without showing up at the dock.

And sometimes when they do show up, they'll eat, but not as aggressively as on other days. "If the bait's not big enough, bass will stay three feet down and watch," Woodard said. "It's like they don't want to waste the energy for a 3-inch shiner."

Other times, they take three or four baits directly from his hand and then back off, waiting for him to toss more to eat. "But if a big bass is still looking at a bait, the smaller ones will stay away," he said. "There's definitely a pecking order."

When a big bass is hungry it can gobble up seven 4-inch brim or a pound (25 count) of shiners.

Not surprisingly, weather can take away their appetite. "They don't seem to like rain and storms (for hand feeding)," Woodard said, adding that maybe they gorge on food washed into the lake by runoff.

"The first day after the rain, they're not hungry. But the second day, they eat."

And finally, there's this for rod-and-reel anglers to ponder: "When I catch a bass and then turn it loose, the others leave with it," Woodard said.

On the other hand, he has caught Jaws and other bass multiple times, and Kickin' Bass is once more coming to the dock for dinner.

Why now?

After catching dozens of big bass by hand over the years, why did Woodard seek notoriety? To help promote his book, which includes bass fishing expertise he acquired fishing all over his home state, and an explanation of how he caught his first bass by hand.

"I had an 8-pounder strike at my thumb while I had my hand in the water after feeding some bass by hand . . . That was fun!" he wrote.

He'd been walking along the shore of a pond during late afternoons, feeding the fish "fiddle worms," when the bass latched onto his thumb. Shocked, he pulled it ashore. Now fast forward a few decades to five years ago, when Woodard retired from teaching and coaching and decided to create "the best bass lake in Alabama," as well as perfect his catching-by-hand technique.

To catch a bass by hand, Woodard explained, you must be certain your thumb goes into the "V" at the bottom of the mouth to ensure a firm grasp. "And you can't pull them out when they're wild," he said. "Bass are very powerful."

Now that he's experienced, 9-pounders just aren't that challenging. But when he latched onto a 12-pounder, "it nearly pulled me under the dock."

And that 16-pounder? "She headed for deep water and pulled me a foot down the pier," the Alabama angler said.

Growing trophy bass

Owners of ponds and small lakes who want to grow bass the size of Woodard's should "step outside the box."

"If you stock bluegill and bass at the traditional 10 to 1 ratio, in two years you'll have an overcrowded pond," said Barry Smith from American Sport Fish Hatchery in Montgomery, Ala., in explaining how to grow double-digit fish. "You'll have too many bass and not enough bluegill."

The 10 to 1 ratio (prey to predator) for stocking, he added, was developed during the 1940s, when the primary objective was to grow harvestable size bass (10 inches) and bluegill (6 inches).

"Instead of 10 to 1, if you go to 20 or even 30 to 1, you'll grow trophy bass," Smith continued. "A bass that is 2 inches in June can be 2 pounds by November.

"People don't realize the growth potential of bass. They are eating machines." And once a bass reaches a pound, he added, it can grow as much as 4 pounds a year. "We have ponds where average growth is 2 pounds and in five years, a bass can weigh 10 to 12 pounds."

No other variables, including genetics, are as important as having abundant forage. "You can't express genetics if you don't have enough food," he said.

Once a fishery managed for trophy bass is established, Smith recommends supplemental stockings of threadfin shad to boost growth even more.

2. Fishing High Water

From the flooded waters of Pickwick Lake, Kentucky pro Bradley Roy brought in about 19 pounds on Day One of an Elite Series tournament.

"It was the perfect storm," he remembered. "The fish had decided to come up to spawn and then the water rose 5 to 6 feet in a week. Those bass shot up like a switch had been turned on.

"In high water sometimes, it's like they're trained," continued the 2010 Rookie of the Year, who caught his fish by flipping. "It doesn't take them long to move up to that shallow cover for food, and especially if they want to spawn."

On Day Two, however, Roy failed to make the cut. What happened?

"I didn't realize how many fish had moved in," he said. "It was hard to believe there would be another fish around a laydown after I'd caught one there the day before. I lost faith in how many bass could be in that area."

Losing faith is even easier for an angler to do when he fails to catch bass. And that's the likely outcome if he moves into flooded waters too soon.

"Bass can move up within 24 hours," said Roy, who's had plenty of experience fishing flood control reservoirs in Kentucky and Tennessee. "But it all depends on the fishery.

"They (bass) want to feel the water is going to stay up awhile before they move up. It could be a day or it could be a week before they're in there (flooded cover)."

Once bass are located, however, fishing high water and following it back down are among the most reliable ways to put a limit in the boat.

That's exactly what happened at Table Rock Lake a few weeks after the Elites Series tournament at Pickwick. More than 13 inches of rain in 72 hours pushed that White River impoundment to historic highs and forced postponement of the Central Open.

But guides there, who experienced a similar situation in years past, found fish even before the high, muddy water filled with debris had peaked.

"The fish were getting ready to spawn," said Tony Weldele, a guide with more than two decades of experience on Table Rock and nearby Taneycomo.

"Some—the smallmouths and spots—stayed where they were and we just had to fish for them in deeper water. Where we had been catching them in 8 to 10 feet of water, we now had to fish in 25 to 30.

"But the largemouths moved right away into the trees and we knew they'd stay put as long as there was 3 to 4 feet of water in there."

Indeed, as a B.A.S.S. Nation Central Divisional revealed, more than a month after the floods, bass were still in the flooded brush. Anglers brought in many 5- and 6-pound largemouths, with a 7-7 as big bass.

But the productive bite that endured through May and into June was about more than just flooded cover, the Table Rock guide said. Flowing water was also a factor. What goes up inevitably comes down, especially in flood-control impoundments, and water pulling out seems to turn on the fish more often than stable or rising water.

Current seems to concentrate the bass in deeper water on points, while falling water, as long as it continues at a moderate pace of a few inches a day, gradually draws fish from the inside edge of cover to the outside and eventually back to their normal depth and range.

Fish aren't predictable as to when or even *if* they'll move into flooded cover. But if they move up, finding them as the water falls generally isn't difficult. By contrast, high water is toughest to fish when it fluctuates. Way up one day, down a little the next, then back up again.

"Fish don't want to have to move in and out," Roy said. "When you've got conditions like that, that's when people struggle the most to find fish."

That's the time for anglers to focus on "anything vertical," the Kentucky pro revealed, adding that bluff walls and floating docks are two of the places he looks for bass when high water is yo-yoing.

"Fish feel like they want to have a comfort zone," he said. "And they can get that in 20 feet of water if they pull off to channel-swing bluff walls or floating docks."

The best walls, he added, are those adjacent to flats with brush.

Additionally, the same strategy can apply if bass have moved up with high water and then a hard pull rapidly drops it out of shoreline cover.

But understanding where fish go as the water rises and falls isn't the only key to success. Knowing when it's going to move up or down also is important.

"If you know when you're going to be fishing, get the phone number of the Corps (or other management agency) for that lake," Roy said. "That way you can find out the times when they're going to release water. If you know before anyone else, it could make a difference."

Baits for high water

If fish stay in the same place they were before the high water, as the smallmouth and spotted bass did on Table Rock Lake in late April and early May, then catching them is more a matter of adjusting than changing tactics. With depth increased by 15 to 20 feet, guides used heavier weights and larger soft plastics to drag across the gravel bottom.

"I like Gitzits and Carolina-rig finesse worms," said guide Tony Weldele. "A swimming grub will work too. You have a lot of choices for these fish."

For largemouths that have moved into shoreline brush, both Weldele and Elites Series pro Bradley Roy opt for flipping jigs and soft plastics and pitching spinnerbaits.

"I like bigger blades that will give me a lot of flash and vibration for big fish," Roy said.

Bass move tight to cover and often are eager to ambush anything that swims by, he added. "You want to be precise and quiet into the water," the pro said. "This is pinpoint fishing to a target."

Weldele added that anglers at Table Rock (and other highland impoundments) don't often get the chance to throw a spinnerbait, primarily because the water is so clear. But with flooded brush and color added by runoff, it becomes one of the most effective baits.

"I was using a spinnerbait to catch bass in people's backyards, along fences and around picnic tables," he said. "For bass, that's just cover to them."

For vertical fishing along bluff walls and around floating docks, Roy recommends a suspending jerkbait or a swimbait. "Throw them parallel to the walls and all around the docks," he said.

ROBERT MONTGOMERY

3. A Word about Technology

A friend who fishes professionally recently called me to voice concerns about young anglers and the future of fishing.

"I want to make the sport stronger," he said. "But I don't think that's what we're doing."

What we're doing, he believes "is moving kids from the couch to the water, but they're still playing games. All they want to do is drive the boat and play with electronics. They need to learn how to fish first, instead of relying on technology."

He sees this more and more in tournaments and believes the problem is compounded by the implied message from industry that owning the latest technology means you'll automatically catch fish.

I couldn't agree more with his assessment. Electronics are useful tools, just like rods, reels, line and lures. But what will you to do when fish are no longer at that spot you marked with your GPS? If you understand bass biology and behavior; if you mapped out migration routes; if you comprehend daily and seasonal movements and the influences of weather; if you can tell what the fish are feeding on and why—then you can figure out where to go and how to catch them. Plus, you get the satisfaction of figuring things out on your own.

Sometimes. As every veteran angler knows, there are no absolutes in fishing.

But understanding the "big picture" of bass fishing will greatly improve your odds. That's why I've written *Kickin' Bass*, and why I wrote my first book, *Better Bass Fishing*.

As a matter of fact, with the help of information contained in both books, I have caught plenty of fish, although, as every angler knows, "plenty" is never enough. You always want to make one more cast and catch one more fish before going in for the day.

---

4. Tailrace Trophies: Fishing Below a Dam

*A*uthor's note: Missouri angler Rick Hart moved to Alabama in 2007 "to do what I live to do: Fish for big smallmouths."

"I soon learned the average angler doesn't just waltz right in and figure a magic solution to put big smallmouths in the boat," he says.

"I learned that what TVA (Tennessee Valley Authority) does with the current coming through the powerhouse or flood gates (of impoundments on the Tennessee River) plays a big role. Good current gets good bites. Once the water is shut down, the fish shut down.

"When water is being pulled by turbines at the dam, the bass know it's feeding time. Threadfin shad are

Rick Hart with a tailrace trophy

on the move or being pulled through and killed by the turbines and making easy meals for smallmouths hiding behind structures."

And Rick learned how to catch big, broad-shoulder bronzebacks that can surpass 7 pounds. Typically, they average 5 pounds or more, and he often catches several lunkers from the same spot. He prefers the tailwaters below Wheeler Dam because the environment there is more "like a lake" than below Pickwick.

Along with catching big bass, he also maintains a popular Facebook fishing page, Rick Hart's TightLines, as well as a website by the same name.

On my first trip with Rick, I caught a 6-pound smallmouth, my personal best. And I caught it on the second cast on a cold, miserable day in April.

Here's Rick to tell you more:

*   *   *   *

While this won't always be the case, as a rule, you won't find big smallmouths by beating the banks with artificials or live bait. Most will be found offshore.

I learned that timing is everything and current is the ticket. One day I pulled up on a spot and caught more than 24 pounds of big smallmouths (5 fish) in 20 minutes. The next day I returned to the same spot and caught more than 27 pounds of largemouths (5 fish), again in 20 minutes, but no smallmouths. On both outings the fish were feeding hard and then quit as fast as they began.

The tailrace (water immediately below the dam) can offer great fishing throughout the year. With experience, you'll know where to start when you see how the current is running. Remember you need to use caution and be aware of your surroundings when fishing below any dam. Listen for sirens that signal changing water conditions through the dam.

There are times when, even though the current is low, a moderate wind can help you drift and pick up a good fish. Also a passing barge can move enough water at times to get a bite.

I am fishing for the biggest smallmouths in the lake. Is there a record smallmouth to be had? I believe so. The best months usually are February through April and October through December.

Most of the big smallmouths will be found offshore, holding on a rockpile or sometimes a hump no bigger than the deck of your boat. Pinpoint casting or drifting is a must.

For drift fishing, I use a split shot rig on light line with a bait hook. Place the split shot about 12 inches to 18 inches above the hook. This is a live-bait application and can be done with either store-bought shiners or bait you've caught with a cast net. Threadfin shad are the preferred forage, but smallmouths also will eat gizzard shad, skipjack herring, and crayfish, as well as other offerings.

When you drift with the current, you want to stay in contact with the bottom, keeping your bait in the strike zone, using a jigging method to bounce off the bottom. Start upstream and drift over prime areas such as rockpiles, humps, gravel bars, and shell mounds.

When choosing a bait, whether it is artificial or live, the amount of current will determine how much weight to use to keep you in touch with the bottom. If you aren't on the bottom, you aren't catching fish.

Big smallmouths like to hang around a seam or break, where the current meets slack water. Another tactic is to sit in the slack water and cast heavy swimbaits, spinnerbaits, or other shad-imitating baits into the current and slow-roll them across the bottom.

I've caught fish using both methods, but prefer live-bait fishing using the drift method. With either tactic, I feel location is the most important factor.

Make sure you have good quality equipment and plain shank hooks for live bait. I like rods that are 7-foot to 7-6 and 10- or 12-pound fluorocarbon line. Some guys may use braid, but I've never had luck with it. And make sure your drag is properly set. You simply can't horse a big smallmouth to the boat. It's a process that requires patience.

Check your line frequently, especially when fishing over rockpiles, shell mounds, and gravel bars.

Keep good records of your trip, including where you caught your fish, water and air temperatures, generating schedules (for water discharges), and cubic feet per second.

Gut feelings have always helped me fish. On some days I've started for the boat ramp and something says, "Stop." On one particular day I had already boated a 6-10 smallmouth with three others of five pounds or more. That's a great day for any angler. But I went with my gut, kept fishing, and caught a 6-12. My personal best smallmouth went 7-2 because I refused to give up on finicky fish that were short-striking the bait.

Taking care of my catches is a main priority. I make sure they go back to the water in great shape.

5. How to Choose a Fishing Guide

*A*s an angler who's traveled the world, John Killian knows bad luck as well as good—and not just with the fishing.
Two time he has fired guides while out on the water.

"I made them take me back to the dock and I walked around until I found other guides," says John, who lives on Lake Wylie in the Carolinas. "Life is way too short and fishing is too much fun to put up with a sorry guide for even an hour."

Killian has become more selective in choosing a fishing guide, but adds that sometimes he still conducts "performance reviews" with his guides.

"I explain that, since I'm paying them, the fish are mine to do whatever I want with," John says. "If I miss a fish or a cast, I appreciate instruction, but not yelling. Fly fishing guides are the worst about this, but usually respond to good, firm performance counseling."

Choosing the right fishing guide for your interests and abilities is another good way to avoid having to conduct "performance counseling." Sometimes, problems and conflicts arise between client and guide because the client hasn't selected wisely. Sometimes the guide is giving the best he can, but it just isn't what the angler anticipated or wants.

"I think the most important thing is to get on the same page with the guide so you both have a good time," Killian continues. "Most of the guides I fish with have become good friends and we've fished together for years."

To help you avoid conflicts and problems and possibly meet guides who will become good friends, I put together the following blueprint for choosing a fishing guide. I relied upon my own experiences with guides, as well as input from some of the best guides around.

First, ask your fishing friends and the guides you know to recommend guides for a specific water or general area you want to fish. That's the best way to get reliable information. If your friend didn't have a good experience, listen carefully to why. But if your best fishing buddy gets back from fishing Lake Fork or Guntersville and tells you it was the worst trip of his life because it rained the entire time and every piece of water was blown out, that's not on the guide.

Next, log on to the internet. "It's always best to fish with a guide you're referred to," says Steve Chaconas, a bass guide on the Potomac River. "But the internet is also a good place to look for a guide. Once you find one, Google the name to see what has been written about him.

"Guides with better reputations might have been written about by magazine writers. If they haven't, it doesn't mean they aren't good. It just means you'll need to check around to find out more about them."

Also, the guide or the outfitter for whom he works will probably maintain a web site. Keeping in mind the type of fishing you prefer, when you want to go, and what species you'd like to catch, read the information provided.

Also look on the web sites for sponsors and recommendations of the guide you're considering.

"We don't endorse someone unless he's highly professional, maintains modern equipment, and has a wonderful reputation," says Dave Burkhardt, owner of Trik Fish, a fishing line company. "One of my established guides, or reps (line salesmen), or I will fish with him to verify his quality, equipment, and knowledge.

"I was burned too many times years ago when I'd go to Florida on vacation with the kids," he adds. "Bad guides make for a less than fun experience."

The big step

Now you're ready to talk to the guide or, if you're heading to a resort outside the country, possibly the owner/operator of the facility. Either e-mail or using the telephone will work, but the best option is to actually meet the guide out on the dock where you also can judge his appearance and attitude, as well as hear what he has to say.

"Look for a guide who loves his job," says Capt. Greg Poland, who guides both offshore and inshore out of the Florida Keys. "But remember we're dealing with nature," he continues. "There are no fences, and the fish move, so don't book a half day of fishing. Give yourself a better chance by fishing a full day. Most of my clients fish a three-day trip."

And what if the fish aren't biting? Sharing the boat with the wrong guide can make for a long, long day.

"The more well educated the guide, the longer the conversation stays interesting," says guide Charles "Chip" Carroll. "Look for guides with knowledge of not only fishing, but also the human and natural history of the surrounding environs. Look for guides who are committed to delivering the same high level of service both on and off the water."

That service could be teaching a technique or how to read the water.

"Some guides aren't very good teachers," Chaconas says. "Some guides might not be able to communicate this, so it's up to the client to ask the right questions to determine whether a guide can handle his skill level."

What questions do you ask?

"This might not be the first, but it should be the deal breaker," says Chaconas. "Ask what form of liability insurance the guide has. If he doesn't have a commercial policy, then you might run into issues. Sometimes, guides will try to cover their business with a regular policy. If the insurance company finds out, it will deny claims in most cases."

For freshwater fishing especially, ask about licenses. It's a small issue before the trip, but could prove major if you're caught on the water without one. Also, how helpful your prospective guide is in dealing with this matter can be an accurate reflection of what's to come.

Good guides and outfitters usually include such information in the itineraries and check lists that they provide.

Here are some other questions:

- Is the guide licensed as required by the state?
- What is the guide's safety record and medical training?
- How many years in business? Some younger guide services can have better customer service and put in more time on the water, attempting to establish a clientele. Yet there is something to be said for longevity, since poor operations go out of business quickly.

- What kind of tackle and gear should you bring and what is provided? This includes clothing, food, and drinks. As with the license, this information should be provided on check lists.

- What kind of fishing does the guide anticipate? The best guides make certain their clients understand the options beforehand. And they do their best to accommodate. "I always like to ask what the client is looking to accomplish out of his or her trip," says Poland. "The worst thing for me as your guide is to go after a trophy fish when all you wanted to do was enjoy a day of bending the rod."

- What happens if the weather doesn't cooperate? Make sure you know Plan B, and maybe even Plan C.

- Are you going to be charged for extras? "Find out before you book," says Chaconas. "There could be a charge for lost lures or for using equipment."

- Alcohol or no alcohol? "If alcohol is important to your trip, you should ask about it," the Potomac guide says. "I don't allow alcohol on my boat, period. Some guides do."

As you're researching, questioning, and considering, keep in mind that guides also can choose their clients. "The clients I enjoy most are the ones who that realize there's much more to the experience than casting a rod and hooking a fish," said guide Telly Evans.

"It's great to see a client stop casting for a moment and enjoy an amazing skyline or be taken aback by the fall colors dancing up a hillside. There is so much more to a fishing trip than just fishing."

ROBERT MONTGOMERY

6. Tackling Northern Lakes

Bass are the same fish whether they're swimming in Alabama's Lake Guntersville or Michigan's Lake Charlevoix. That means the same baits and techniques will work wherever you pursue them.

But don't make the mistake of thinking that natural lakes of the northern U.S. and Canada, including the Great Lakes and many of the fisheries from Minnesota across to New England, should be approached in the same way as the manmade impoundments many of us call our home waters. Yes, the fish are the same—but their environments are not.

I asked experts on northern waters to explain differences between the two types of fisheries and reveal how they catch fish in the natural lakes on both sides of the U.S./Canada border.

"For those who haven't tried fishing on a northern natural lake, I think they'd be in for a real treat," said Mike Desforges, an Ontario guide and pro.

"You may not catch a 10-pound bass on a northern lake," he added. "But the numbers of fish in the 3- to 5-pound class will make up for it."

Bernie Schultz, a frequent Bassmaster Classic qualifier who has won events in both Canada and New York, added, "I prefer northern lakes when the weather is agreeable. And once you find fish, they usually stay put for a while. Too often, that isn't the case on southern lakes or impoundments."

That's because those reservoir bass often follow bait, while northern bass do not, Desforges explained.

"I believe on natural lakes the bass set up on good structure or cover and wait for the feed to come to them," he said. "Even open-water smallmouths 'chasing' bait don't really chase bait. They more or less rise off the bottom and always seem to relate to the bottom structure even if they're suspended in open water."

Differences in physical characteristics of the fisheries also contribute to this difference, Shultz said. Reservoirs contain submerged roadbeds, bridges, "and other underwater structures that were once part of a landscape above water level."

"A lot of the structure you fish on impoundments is either manmade or is somehow related to currents, creek channels, and ledges," Desforges explained. "You don't find much of that on natural lakes.

"On natural lakes, most fish relate to natural shoreline cover, offshore weedlines, rock humps, points, bars, or just changes in bottom composition."

Clarity is yet another difference, with 10 to 15 feet visibility being common on northern waters, and 25 to 30 feet a possibility. By contrast, you rarely can see more than 5 feet in many reservoirs.

"The difference in water clarity has an effect on bait selection," Desforges said. "Smaller profile soft plastics are top choices under most conditions on northern lakes. And using fluorocarbon line will get you more bites."

But, the Canadian angler cautioned, sometimes you should muscle up when going after big smallmouth bass.

"Speed often makes big smallmouths stupid," he said. "The same fish that seemed finicky and turned its nose at your small lifelike bait will often turn around and smash a big ¾-ounce chartreuse spinnerbait burned by them, or a 6-inch jerkbait retrieved as erratically as possible. Other great choices for reaction strikes are top waters and 4- to 5-inch swimbaits."

Schultz revealed that he often uses his northern water strategies for largemouth bass on the natural lakes of Florida.

"I look for grass, docks, and other shallow features first," he said. "If I'm after largemouths, grass and docks are primary. For smallmouths, rocky shoals or fields of broken rock mixed with grass are ideal, so long as the depth is adequate."

Depth depends on time of year, he added, explaining that smallies are often shallow. "Other times, you find them deep. But the cover or structure is often the same. And don't forget the forage. Finding the right forage means finding bass."

Shallow doesn't necessarily mean near shore either. "Except during the spawn, smallmouths tend to use more offshore structures such as points, sunken islands, and sand bars," Desforges said. "Finding the spot on the spot is important for largemouths, but when dealing with smallies, 10 or 15 feet can make the difference between catching a boat load of big bass and catching nothing." The key, he added, is to locate something different, such as the highest spot on a rockpile, the transition area from one type of bottom to another, or a small piece of vegetation on a sand or boulder flat.

Also for offshore smallies, start your search at the same depth as the water clarity and then double that number. For example, if clarity is to 10 feet, then search depths of 10 to 20 feet.

Largemouths, by contrast, like a "roof" over them, said Desforges, adding that might mean fallen trees, lily pads, weed mats, undercut banks, docks, swim platforms, or tire walls.

He also believes shallow can be good for largemouths in northern waters most any time, from spring through fall, because of lack of fishing pressure. Couple that lack of pressure with a shorter growing season, and northern bass often are more ready to bite when you find them, Schultz said.

"Smallmouths are probably the biggest reason to travel north," he continued. "They're fun and it seems their size and numbers are increasing on many northern lakes."

But be careful in pursuing them, the Florida angler emphasized. "Winds can gust in a hurry and with that comes big waves, especially on the Great Lakes. If you get caught in rough conditions, take your time and negotiate each wave as it approaches. Getting in a hurry will only lead to disaster."

Planning a trip

Most any time from May through mid October can be good for bass fishing in northern waters, according to David Rose, owner of WildFishing Guide Service near Traverse City, Mich. But he doesn't recommend July. "That's post spawn and the fish are full because of major bug hatches," he said.

Guiding mainly for smallmouth bass, Rose said that 5- to 7-pound fish are real possibilities in northern waters, with one of his clients boating an 8 ½-pound behemoth.

The spring bite typically begins as water creeps up to 55 degrees, he explained. Smallies feed heavily on steep breaklines, with jerkbaits among the most productive offerings.

That pattern will continue until the water rises about another 10 degrees and the fish start to move shallow. "On bright, warm days, you might see them up on flats," Rose said. "But they don't always stay there."

Shallow fish will hit creature baits, lizards, and tubes. Spinnerbaits and jerkbaits are other options, especially when searching for fish.

By late June, bugs start to hatch and smallmouth bass begin gorging themselves. Clear-pattern Pop Rs and Spooks that imitate fluttering on the surface sometimes fool fish.

As smallies grow hungry again, they cruise. "You might catch them in 5 feet or 65 feet," the guide said. "Some tend to go to the same breaklines they were on in the spring.

"I like to put my boat in 8 to 10 feet of water so I can cast shallow or deep. I use a lot of search baits, with topwaters early and late. You can catch smallmouths on top over 30 feet of water."

When the water cools, fish will follow forage into shallower water, with crawfish abundant into October and then minnows dominating.

ROBERT MONTGOMERY

7. Seeing Spots: The Joy of
Spotted Bass

When Mike Bucca goes fishing, he sees spots.

But it's an addiction, not an affliction.

While spotted bass are an incidental catch for many anglers, the guide specifically targets them in north Georgia lakes such as Lanier, Carters, and Allatoona, where they predominate. What Mike has learned about spotted bass and the success he enjoys pursuing them might convince you to target them.

And in ways you've never considered.

"Most people fail to realize that spotted bass are twice as aggressive as largemouth, and it's the same with curiosity," said Bucca. "Those are the number one aspects any angler can capitalize on and turn to his advantage."

This Georgia guide learned about spots from assisting with electrofishing surveys as well as catching them. He employs a run-and-gun, power offense most of the time, whether he's throwing a tube with a trailer treble for short bites, a suspending jerkbait, or (preferably) an 8-inch Bull Shad swimbait Bucca makes himself.

Mike Bucca with a spotted bass

That's right. His go-to bait for spotted bass, a fish that rarely exceeds 6 pounds, is a huge lure usually reserved for targeting double-digit largemouths in Mexico, California, and Texas.

"I noticed from electrofishing that we caught a lot of 4- and 5-pound spots with big, forked gizzard shad tails sticking out of their gullets," Mike said. "We also noticed a lack of smaller shad. My theory is, the meal-sized shad get eaten before they get too big."

After repeatedly, seeing this behavior, Bucca realized the smaller swimbaits he bought and used weren't necessarily the best choice for catching smaller, but more curious and aggressive spotted bass. Generally, these baits were trout imitators designed for throwing to West Coast bass, which often feed on stocked rainbow trout.

"Until recently, there were no big gizzard-shad-type baits or big threadfin- or blueback-herring-profile baits," the guide said. "And that's what spotted bass feed on."

So he created the Bull Shad. And spots, from two pounds to more than six, have proven most appreciative, with late winter through the spawn being prime time and fall a close second. Bucca even has caught crappie on the huge lures.

"I like the big swimbait because it's an absolute rush to watch a giant spot attack it," explains the Georgia angler, who keeps the jointed lure on top or near the surface with a speedy retrieve. "Topwater can't even come close to the rush you get on a big swimbait bite."

Bucca asserts swimbait fishing is "the least understood technique in all of bass fishing, especially in the South." Also, the larger ones, he insists, are *not* too big for spotted bass and mid-size largemouths, contrary to what many anglers believe.

However, these larger baits do require specialized tackle to utilize properly. The Georgia angler likes long, stout rods with some flex in the tips, as well as heavy duty reels and 25-pound line. When you're casting 4-ounce baits over and over again, you need a line that can take some serious abuse," he said.

One of the main reasons the baits work, he believes, is that so few people use them, especially on heavily pressured fisheries where anglers tend to downsize baits instead of upgrade.

Another is that a swimbait mimics a large, easy meal. "Bass, especially big bass, are efficient feeders," he said. "They would rather eat one big meal instead of exerting a lot of energy eating a bunch of small meals."

Georgia fisheries biologist Jim Hakala added, "If a large prey is acting normally, the trigger to strike may not be there. But if something large isn't acting right, they make take the opportunity to hammer it. And I think a lot of times they (bass) select for a certain size prey that is usually much smaller than what they can handle.

Downsizing

While Bucca's preferred method for catching spots is to throw big baits traditionally associated with trophy largemouths, he shifts to the opposite extreme during winter. That's when he goes with the float-and-fly, a finesse method popularized by smallmouth anglers on Dale Hollow and other Tennessee/Kentucky lakes.

He starts fishing the small jig below a float as the water drops into the low 50s and sticks with that bait until the temperature starts to rise past 55 in early spring.

"I concentrate more on the float-and-fly after a hard (cold) front passes through," he said. "That really makes the fish suspend and inactive and requires a very slow presentation."

He twitches the small shad-imitation along bluff walls or 45-degree sloping banks and gradually moves more to the main lake as winter comes on.

"It (float-and-fly) is at its strongest first thing in the morning and gets weaker as the day progresses," said Bucca, adding that following the shade is a good way to prolong the pattern.

"Plan your strategy around the sun and fish along walls that don't have much of a shade line first. Then work your way toward the bluffs that have the most shade," he said.

"This is a lethal technique from late fall to late winter for trophy spotted bass."

Where are they?

In lakes they share, spotted bass can be found in the same locations as largemouths. But they are decidedly different fish.

"The biggest difference between the two species is habitat," said guide Mike Bucca. "Largemouths are basically shallow-water fish that love wood. Spots are much more adaptive, as they can be just as happy in shallow, woody environment as they are in deep, clear environment with absolutely no cover or structure."

Look for spots, he advises, around points—especially main lake points—bluff walls, and rocky shorelines. And don't forget they often suspend.

In general, spotted bass will be deeper than largemouths, added Norm Klayman, a former tournament angler and guide who has been catching both species on Bull Shoals for more than 40 years. "Once they get past the spawn, they will move deeper faster than largemouths," he added. "Sometimes, they run open water over channels and you can catch them on top."

While largemouths like flats, Klayman said, spots tend to prefer larger rocks and hang out more along channels, especially at the ends of bluffs and chunk-rock banks.

Spot specifics

- The world record spotted bass weighed 11-4 and was caught in 2017 at New Bullards Bar Reservoir, Calif. The previous record of 10-6 came from the same fishery in 2015.
- Smith Lake in Alabama yielded the 20-pound test record (8-10) in 1972, but all other line-class records have some from Pine Flat and Perris, both in California, where the spotted bass, like the largemouth, is an introduced species.
- The original range for spotted bass extended from east Texas to Alabama and up into the drainages of the Mississippi and Ohio rivers.
- Spotted bass include at least two subspecies: Alabama and northern, also known as Kentucky spotted bass or just "Kentucky."
- Spotted bass are believed to be less cold tolerant than smallmouths and largemouths.

- The name for spotted bass is derived from their scale coloring below the lateral line.
- Although they seem to have smaller mouths and brighter color than largemouths, spotted bass are more accurately identified by a rough "tooth" patch on the tongue.

---

8. California Girls

*A*uthor's note: The big bass lakes of southern California are unique. Deep, clear, and heavily fished, they are stocked with Florida strain bass that grow large and fat, usually because they feed on stocked rainbow trout. In fact, the *San Diego Fish* website reports that 11 of the biggest largemouth bass of all time were caught in San Diego County.

Additionally, anglers who pursue these "California girls" are often at the forefront of innovation. For example, they were throwing swimbaits long before anglers in the rest of the country. Spybaits are another bait they pioneered.

That being the case, I asked my friend Pat Helsley to explain how it's done, because he's been fishing these waters for decades. All of his double-digit bass, including a 13-5, came on a

Pat Helsley with a California bass

jig. In the 7- to 9-pound range, he's caught "too many to count," mostly on jigs and Texas-rig plastics.

Here's Pat to tell you more:

*   *   *   *   *

Winter baits include 1/2-ounce football jigs, drop shots with Roboworms, Texas rigs, swimbaits, underspins, 10-inch worms on standup jigheads, and Ned rigs. Also try green pumpkin/black flake skirts and trailers and other plastics, as well as worms in pumpkin, pink, and purple.

For the most part, bass are going to be 30 to 80 feet deep, depending on the lake. I look for humps, deep ledges, rock piles, dams, and main lake points.

Fish these baits slowly! Florida strain bass are lazy in cold water. Let your jig hit bottom and sit for a moment. Then slowly start crawling it. Keep it in constant contact with the bottom. Only hop it enough to get over an obstacle.

I dead stick jigs and Texas rigs quite a bit.

California stocks these lakes with trout so throw those swimbaits!

Let underspins hit the bottom like a dying shad. Then moderately pull up. Basically just lift your rod from the water up to your shoulders, then let it drop. Do this a few times, then slowly reel it back to the boat, occasionally letting it drop back to the bottom.

I put a 10-inch worm on a standup jig head and then just wiggle it. Reel in a turn or two and then wiggle it again. Repeat this all the way back to the boat. This is a big fish bait and technique.

Prespawn and post spawn baits include jerkbaits, spinnerbaits, crankbaits, small swimbaits, spybaits, Senkos, and jigs and Texas rigs.

Hit secondary points, creek bends, and the edges of flats where the fish are schooling up to bed or to return to offshore structure for the summer. Keep changing your cadence and technique until you find what they want. With jigs and Texas rigs, find ledges and rocks, pop them off them and swim the baits a few feet, or just let them fall off.

Due to huge pressure on these small lakes, I don't intentionally fish the beds. But if you get a Brush Hawg on a Texas rig near a bed, a bass will destroy it, much as it would take a lizard.

At this time of year I switch all my creature baits to watermelon black/red flake and use this color combo through fall. Jig skirts are green pumpkin and orange with black/ red flake. One more thing: throw bluegill baits. Bass love to hate them because they are bed raiders.

Summer is smorgasbord time. Senkos, shallow squarebills, medium and deep diving crankbaits, swimbaits, jigs, Texas rigs, rats, frogs, and worms, all are good.

Fish are found at every level from shallow to deep. Attract them with reaction baits, and throw in the creatures while you're at it. The big girls will move off the banks and suspend or stay on the bottom. Once you find them, simply find the cadence and technique that will get them to bite, which is just about anything. These bass are hungry and willing. In early morning use topwaters, walkers, wake baits, and other reaction baits until the lights come on bright. Then go to creature baits. Frogs work on the grass canopies all day. Find ledges, walls, rockpiles, tules, and brush when it's bright out, anything that fish can find shade behind or in. Throw a skirted punch bait.

Because our water is gin clear 90 percent of the time, I use natural colors as much as possible, with the exception of worms. For some reason, pink worms like the Folkestad special work until the sun is up high. Then I go to green pumpkin, watermelon or oxblood red flake, all straight tails.

In fall, throw topwater and swimmers, especially shad imitations. Spinnerbaits, Senkos, and jigs are still in the game as well. Swim those jigs or move them fast on the bottom. Bluegill swimbaits are good too.

Due to horribly bad shoulders I can't throw the big swimbaits, so I throw big jigs for lunkers. They are a minimum 5 to 6 inches in length and I believe they intimidate smaller bass, as I rarely catch them on it.

I like to use an orange trailer. It starts out as a watermelon black/red flake and I get the color change by setting it in the sun. The Yamamoto watermelon color is the only one that will change colors like that. If you set a bag of them in the sun, they will change from green to red and then to orange. I do this with both the Flappin' Hawgs and the twintail Hula grubs. If you put a full bag of them in the sun, in which they are mixed together, they will marble, parts of them reddish and parts of them green. This is a dynamite trick that really catches a fish's eye. If you spread them out, they change colors evenly and solidly. The longer they're exposed, the more they change, eventually becoming orange.

---

9. Great Lakes Bronzebacks

*A*uthor's note: A while back, I experienced an extraordinary day of fishing for smallmouth bass with Capt. Dale Stroschein on Lake Michigan. He's the owner of Wacky Walleye Guide Service and a member of the Freshwater Fishing Hall of Fame.

That day was so good, in fact, that I wrote about it for my book *Why We Fish* and headlined the story "The Best Day." Here's an excerpt:

*   *   *   *   *

Dale Stroschein with a Great Lakes bronzeback

The *smaller* ones were 3 pounds, and we weighed several that checked in at 5 ½ pounds or more. Doubles were common, and we often caught three, four, or even five fish on successive casts. We didn't keep count, but we certainly caught more than 50 quality smallmouths in just three to four hours of fishing.

Even for my veteran guide, the bite was extraordinary. He took a break from the action to call a friend and tell him about it.

As the bite finally slowed a bit, Dale wrestled a smallmouth that clobbered a topwater while I battled another on a spinnerbait. When his fish neared the boat, I grabbed the net with one hand as I clung to my rod with the other.

His was a huge bass, possibly 7 pounds or better, and definitely the biggest fish of the day. If it had been hooked on a spinnerbait, we might have landed it. But as the bass thrashed and tailwalked all over the surface, it was connected to Dale's line only with the tenuous treble of a topwater. And when I reached out to stick the net under the fish, the frame touched it, sending the bronzeback into even more violent spasms.

In a heartbeat, it was gone.

On any other day losing a bass like that might have ruined our day, and, for me it did create a slight blemish. I hate making a mistake when trying to net a friend's fish.

But we both were thoroughly exhausted and exhilarated by the near non-stop action from fierce, broad-shouldered smallmouths that, for some reason, had stacked up in that shallow little cove. And a thunderstorm was moving in.

*　　*　　*　　*　　*

That's why I asked Dale to share his knowledge about how to catch bronzebacks in Green Bay and Lake Michigan specifically and the Great Lakes generally. Especially pay attention to what he says about the wind. Wind was the primary reason we fished the cove on that remarkable day. And it's always a key factor when fishing big waters. Here's Dale:

*   *   *   *   *

Make sure you pay close attention to the winds. South/east winds on the west side of the Door Peninsula (Green Bay) will lower water temperatures and make for difficult fishing. But you have the luxury of going on the lake side of the Door County area, where conditions shouldn't be affected and you'll be fine. The same goes for north/west winds on the east side, which is Lake Michigan. Water temperatures will drop as much as 10 to 15 degrees and fish won't return for many days to the bays on the Lake Michigan side.

Work the wind-blown shorelines. Having some wind on the water often leads to a more productive day. On nine out of ten windy days, you'll see better quality and higher numbers of fish. Both hard-body baits and plastic will work. On calm days, you'll typically do best with plastic.

On calm days, you won't catch as many fish if you work your bait all the way back to the boat. On these crystal clear waters, when you see the fish, they see you. Once they see you, they won't bite. On calm days, work the bait halfway back to the boat and then reel up to make another cast. On many days, you'll get bit as soon as the bait hits the water.

The waters of Lake Michigan and Green Bay are crystal clear, with visibility often as deep as 30 to 40 feet. It's imperative to make long casts and use fluorocarbon line as a leader.

Keep moving until you contact fish. If you're drifting along the shoreline, do not go back and drift the same section again. In this clear water you'll catch the majority of fish on the first pass through. Make the most of your time by moving on to the next location right away.

The best depths and locations to increase your catch are somewhat dependent on the time of year. For example, from our opening day on May 1 until the latter part of June, you'll find the most fish in 10 feet of water or less, nestled nicely in the bays up and down the peninsula of Door County. By July many of the fish finish spawning and begin the transition to open water shorelines outside of the bays, offshore structures, and islands that guard the Door Peninsula. Fish will stay in areas like Monument Shoal, Sisters Shoal, Hat Island, Adventure Island, Spider Island, and Chambers Island—in depths of 10 to 30 feet—until late fall.

One of the best bites on Lake Michigan in July will be on and around Washington Island, which opens for the season on the first Saturday of July. This area remains closed for an extended time, allowing fish to spawn without angling pressure. All the tips I've talked about will apply to this special place.

September, October, and November are the best months to target Lake Michigan and Green Bay. During this time fish are binging hard to build up fat to survive the winter. You'll see more trophy fish and experience hardly any angling pressure.

Super lines, such as Berkley Fireline, work exceptionally well. They should be accompanied by fluorocarbon leaders as long as six feet. You'll cast farther with this combination and catch more fish.

Square bills, stick baits, lipless lures, and small diving baits are great choices for hard-body baits.

If you use spinnerbaits, go heavy: 3/4-ounce and more. They work well for long casts. Keep them in the top one foot of the water column for more bites.

Good choices for finesse baits include wacky worm, Ned rig, hair jigs, tubes, drop shot, and twister tails.

Finally, please protect our natural resources wherever you fish. Bass brought up from more than 35 feet typically won't survive as well as those caught in shallower water. Fish that are 6, 7, and up to 8 pounds take many years to grow that large. Also, if you decide to harvest a fish, please use good judgment to help protect our resources. Finally, if a fish is deep hooked, it's best to cut the line and release it in hopes that it will see another day.

ROBERT MONTGOMERY

---

10. Tidal River Bass

*A*uthor's note: Capt. Steve Chaconas is a premiere guide on one of the nation's best known bass fisheries, the Potomac River. It also happens to be a tidal river fishery, which means rising and falling waters daily. An angler needs specialized knowledge to consistently catch fish in such waters—and that's why I asked Steve, a long-time friend and owner of National Bass Guide Service, to share what he's learned over the years.

Steve also contributed to my other books, including *Why We Fish* and *Fish, Frogs, and Fireflies*. Here is his take on fishing the Potomac:

Steve Chaconas with tidal river bass

*   *   *   *   *

For a variety of reasons, tidal fishing can spook anglers more that the bass. Many people are intimidated when they launch their boats and a few hours later the water level changes from 3 to 8 feet in many areas.

The tidal influence positions fish according to the cover and proximity to a channel. As long as there's about a foot of water, at low tide fish will stay with the cover. As FLW pro Bill Chapman once said when fishing in water only 6 inches deep, "The fish I'm after aren't all that tall."

But tides confuse newcomers to the Potomac and other tidal rivers. Simply put, you should move in with the tide and out with the tide. Be in your best spot during the last two hours of falling tides.

Also, current flows in two directions and fish reposition throughout the day. Even the intensity of the flow impacts fish. Wind will force the water to drop faster and even lower than normal, leaving many fishing spots high and dry.

By their nature, tidal systems connect to saltwater bodies. This intrusion can impact the areas during wet or very dry seasons. Weather and changing tides may kill submerged vegetation and force fish to seek fresher confines. Excessive rainfall or flooding brings more fresh water and fish move into previously barren spots.

In simple terms, when tides come in, fish move up toward shore cover. When tides drop, fish seek deeper grass edges or scattered cover. In-between tides require a lot of practice and experience to navigate.

But on the plus side, tidal fisheries are fishable nearly year round as they rarely ice over. Out of the current, deeper areas are winter homes for bass. Warmer temperatures move bass to shallow flats, creek bends, and channels, often to feed on shad or crawfish.

And then there's the grass factor. Find the grass and chances are you'll find the bass. For most anglers, all grass is hydrilla. Not that it matters, but there are several other species.

In reality, hydrilla is the most difficult to fish, as it creates a thick, horizontal carpet to shield bass from lures. It clears the water and provides habitat, which helps fry become yearlings.

On the Potomac, hydrilla was a pioneer grass, clearing the way for other grasses like coontail, water celery, star grass, and milfoil to become established. Timing is everything and milfoil is right on time. It remains dormant during the low sunlight winter months and emerges at the beginning of March, just in time for prespawn and the spawn. Architecturally different from hydrilla, it grows in small vertical clumps, providing a base for spawning and tall cover for ambush feeding. Milfoil is the best grass. When it's around, bass are there. When it dies off, bass vacate.

Spadderdock pads also can hold bass. On the Potomac, these pad fields are best along creek channels when the tide is going out, and in bays when the tide is going in. When water is falling, fish at the edge and into the channel. Larger pad fields in bays are better with more water as fish move into them. The first hour or two of falling tide is best in these areas.

Just about any lure from June to November will work at the right place at the right tide in and near pads. Buzzbaits, toad style baits, and hollow frogs can cover deep into the pad fields. Jigs and Texas-rigged soft plastics can be used to pick out specific pad targets like irregularities, points, and other cover embedded in the pads.

Bait choice and color often depend on water clarity, and tidal river water clarity is always changing. It also varies by season. In the cold-water months, water can have 3 to 5 feet of visibility. On the Potomac, warm-water discharge areas like Blue Plains in Washington, D.C., Four Mile Run, and Possum Point in Virginia, the water may be clear down to 10 feet or more. These areas are also up to 15 degrees warmer, staying around 50 degrees in the coldest months. Tides carry warmed water to adjacent areas.

Throughout the year, grass beds filter sediment, absorb nutrients, and help with water clarity. Boat wake and wind can muddy these areas as grass is agitated, dropping the plants' trapped silt. Excessive winds pounding shorelines can render entire bays nearly unfishable. Heavy spring rains allow headwaters to muddy tidal waters. Anglers paying attention to daily trends can predict conditions in their spots, knowing that either an incoming or outdoing tide can change clarity.

The Potomac is a shallow fishery. Grass grows in depths up to 5 feet. The advent of braid sent bass fishing leapfrogging into a new dimension. Bass previously unreachable with conventional techniques now attacked frogs. Braid allows longer casts, instant hook sets, and the strength to horse big fish out of heavy grass cover.

Frogs can provide an all-day bite on the river. At high tide the frog makes a great search bait. At lower tides in the middle of the day, it can provide some hefty fish.

Slow rolling spinnerbaits and throwing Mann's Baby 1-Minus have remained mainstays on the Potomac. Suspending jerkbaits, the 100 sizes, in clown patterns will work when water is above 50 degrees. Deeper running crankbaits in red patterns around grass and wood cover brings results during the typically high spring waters. Using 10- to 12-pound fluorocarbon line allows the baits to be worked slowly, while staying in the strike zone.

Soft plastics, jigs, and swim jigs come into play in April and May as grass beds begin to develop edges and holes. They should be rigged Texas-style and fished with 12- or 14-pound fluorocarbon. Use light weights, 1/8-ounce and up as needed. I prefer unpegged to give the tubes a bit more action when the weight separates.

Pitch to multiple clumps in a group, thick individual clumps, and into holes between clumps. Pitch into the current and vary presentations along the side of clumps.

Black and blue jigs also work during this period as well.

Topwaters start drawing bites in early June, once the water clears and stays around 70. Post-spawn bass will take walking lures. Poppers can be worked over grass at high tides, along edges at low, and into holes at other times.

Stickworms can be productive from April into October. Fish them weightless with a 3/0 offset wide-gap worm hook and a small bullet weight, or even as a shaky head.

In the fall, grass beds begin to break up, as days are shorter and the water cools, causing plants to die or go dormant. Until the water falls below 50 degrees, fish are still shallow on grass remnants or hard cover. This is a perfect crankbait opportunity.

This dwindling cover provides the angling version of musical chairs. As cover drops out, fish congregate on what's left. Tossing a variety of lures, even poppers, that get close to the fish will produce.

For poppers, however, conditions need to be almost perfect. Overcast skies, with calm, clear, and low water over cover are ideal. You should also have feathered rear trebles hooks.

A pop of the lure followed by a pause until still, followed by a slight gentle pull, not a pop, will entice fish to reveal their presence. Watch the bait for any movement as fish maneuver under the lure to take a look. If they do, a slight pull will allow the feathered treble to rise and when stopped, the feather will drop and open slowly to encourage a reluctant bite.

As winter sets in, a handful of lures will keep you busy as you target steep drops and out-of-the-current areas. Silver Buddy's blade bait will not only cover water, but reveal the depth and mood of fish. Other good winter choices include 3-inch tubes with ¼-ounce insert heads and 3-inch avocado Stingray grubs on a ¼-ounce ball head jig.

A little history of the Potomac

Few people are Washington, D.C. natives, but my dad was born and raised in the nation's capital. That meant he grew up fishing the Potomac. He knew all the spots for catfish, yellow perch, and the famous shad runs. Angling in the '40s, '50s and into the '60s didn't produce many largemouth bass. Angling for bass didn't begin to take off until 1970s.

My dad took Air Force assignments in Turkey and in Alabama from 1963 to 1969, so we didn't see what was happening to the river. When we returned, we saw trash, well-worn paths overgrown with brush, and health department warning signs. The water had become so contaminated that contact with it could result in a visit to the emergency room. A century of neglect turned the once bountiful Potomac into an open sewer.

In signing the Water Quality Act of 1965, President Lyndon Johnson said, "We must act, and act swiftly. The hour is late, the damage is large."

He added that two hundred years ago, George Washington stood on his lawn at Mount Vernon and viewed a river that was clean and sweet and pure. He pointed out that President Theodore Roosevelt used to swim in the Potomac.

"But today the Potomac is a river of decaying sewage and rotten algae. Today all the swimmers are gone; they have been driven from its banks."

Fortunately, President Johnson's signature to clean the water had an immediate impact. Within ten years, water quality improved and awareness kept trash out of the river. By the mid '70s, our river had visibly improved.

Today, the tidal Potomac is one of the most visited fisheries in the country by both recreational and tournament anglers of all levels. Additionally, major bass tours make frequent stops there, often with several events annually. Primary launch areas are Leesylvania on the Virginia shore and Smallwood State Park in Maryland, with another half dozen or so smaller ramps along the river.

11. What I Learned in Mexico

For more than a decade I fished Lake El Salto and other Mexico fisheries at least once a year, and sometimes two or three times a year. I felt blessed to have the opportunity and will be forever grateful to Billy Chapman of Anglers Inn for his generous hospitality.

For 99 percent of fishermen, a double-digit bass is the fish of a lifetime. I caught ten of them in Mexico, mostly on El Salto, along with hundreds of 7- to 9-pound fish. I say this not to brag, but to put into perspective what I observed—and what I hope will help make you a better bass angler. After all, bass are bass wherever they live. Here's what I learned in Mexico:

1. There really is something to the idea that fish—especially big bass—are more susceptible to a bait they've never have seen before. If a bait you've had lots of luck with stops being productive, try offering a smaller version to the fish.

On our first trip to El Salto, my friend and I caught more than 150 bass the first day, mostly on common topwaters such as the Zara Spook and all in the 2- to 4-pound range. Lots of fun, but no big fish. The same pattern continued for the next three days.

Then, on the night before we left we had dinner with an Oklahoma angler who'd been catching big bass. In fact, that was almost all that he caught. And he was catching them on a magnum Fat Free Citrus Shad crankbait. He gave me one of them.

One the afternoon of the final day, as my friend relaxed and fished soft plastics, I threw the crankbait. Just a few casts in, I hooked and boated a 12-4, which tied with a bass I caught at Lake Guerrero as my largest ever. Several other bass followed, all more than 5 pounds.

When we returned about the same time the next year, the pattern still held. But on this trip we had plenty of time to throw that magic bait. Of the 13 double-digit bass we caught, 10 of them came on the crankbait, topped by a 14-8. We took the other three on an Offset Sam, a topwater with unusual action and a bait those Mexico bass had almost certainly never seen. And we caught few bass, if any, under 5 pounds on the crankbait.

On our third trip it all changed. Big bass weren't nearly as aggressive as in the past, while smaller fish eagerly went after the crankbait, possibly because they no longer were losing out to the lunkers.

Not long after, a similar pattern followed with the Storm WildEye Swim Shad. At first big bass gobbled up the 6-inch version. As they became accustomed to that, anglers switched to 5-inch and continued catching fish. Finally bass of all sizes mostly ignored the larger baits and would strike only the 4-inch.

2. Don't overlook the tops of trees. Birds aren't the only critters you might find there.

On that second trip to El Salto we had an all-day downpour, a rarity for that time of year. Incredibly, my friend and I were the only ones in camp who brought rainsuits. Everyone else donned garbage-bag ponchos, but quickly learned they provided little relief and beat a hasty retreat to camp.

My friend and I had the lake to ourselves and enjoyed one of the best days of fishing in our lives. Yes, we threw that Citrus Shad crankbait, but now the fish weren't deep, as they had been during fair weather. They were in the tops of flooded trees. All we had to do was cast near branches, make a crank or two, and hold on. But they wouldn't hit a topwater.

I caught a 5 and a 7 on one cast during that crazy day, and often we saw other bass following the ones we hooked. My friend connected with one so heavy he couldn't stop it and it eventually pulled free. He's a skilled angler, too, having caught bass up to 15 pounds in Florida. Was that bass a world record? We'll never know.

Was rain the reason big bass moved into the tree tops? I think so. But the point is, the fish were in water 15 to 20 feet deep, but holding adjacent to vertical cover just a few feet below the surface, and they ate only when we pulled the bait in front of them.

3. If you want to fish in the afternoon, don't drink margaritas at lunch.

Well . . . maybe just one.

4. A temperature drop of only a degree or two can make a big difference in the bite, especially for Florida strain bass.

We saw this consistently, especially during late fall and winter. Yes, bass bit during cool weather. But a drop temporarily turned them off. The saving grace was that, as the temperature rose during the day, the bite heated up as well.

5. Many anglers don't research and prepare properly. As a perfect example of that, I give you people who spend big bucks to go fishing in Mexico, but don't take foul weather gear in case it rains.

I remember other examples. Some fishermen brought spinning reels, two-piece buggy whip rods, and 10-pound line to pursue big bass. Their chances of catching one with such equipment were slim and none. Others rigged big plastics Texas-style with hooks way too small to penetrate the bait, much less the jaw of a lunker.

6. When spending time at any remote camp or lodge, especially in Mexico and other countries with warm climates, be ever vigilant for critters in your quarters.

Check your shoes before putting them on in the morning. If you don't, you might mash flat a harmless little lizard. You also might get stung by a scorpion.

Also look twice before stepping into the shower. A couple of times, I've found the stall already occupied by uninvited guests. And at night, don't walk to the bathroom barefooted.

7. In hot weather, plastics fished slowly are usually the best option. That isn't a new revelation for veteran anglers, but the point was driven home to me while fishing El Salto during summer.

The warmer the water, the faster the metabolism for cold-blooded bass, and the more they must eat to sustain themselves. But the warm water also affords less oxygen than cooler water, meaning bass inherently prefer to expend as little energy as possible to feed.

On one brutally hot June day I caught a 10-13, a bass with a huge head, but skinny stomach. Knowing how fragile big fish can be during such conditions, I quickly brought the bass to the boat, weighed it, and released it. Total time out of water was less than 30 seconds. Still, I had to work with the fish for a minute or so to revive it because that brief struggle exhausted it.

---

12. Hydrilla or Milfoil: Which Is Better?

*A*sk most any bass angler about hydrilla and Eurasian water-milfoil and he can tell you they are "grass" and they attract bass. But they are not the same plant, and knowing which is which and when one is better than the other will help you catch more fish.

Ask him to explain the difference between the two and he probably can't – unless he's a pro or he fishes Sam Rayburn, Guntersville, or other reservoirs that contain both grasses.

Pros know the difference because their success sometimes depends on it.. Knowing when and why can be the difference between finishing in or out of the money. That also means they don't always want to tell you what plant held their fish, preferring instead to just say "grass."

Hydrilla

"No matter where we go, the lake that offers either or both is always better than a lake that doesn't," said Todd Faircloth, a pro from Texas who uses his knowledge of plants and their differences to his advantage.

Knowing more about them can help you catch bass too, whether you already fish a reservoir with hydrilla and milfoil, or you plan to visit a fishery with one or both.

Distribution

Milfoil is native to Europe, Asia, and northern Africa, and likely was accidentally introduced in the nursery trade during late 19th or early 20th century. Hydrilla originated in Asia, and was brought in as an aquarium plant during the 1950s. Milfoil is the more widely distributed, while hydrilla is mostly in the South, across to California.

"Eurasian water-milfoil is present in most U.S. states and in British Columbia, Ontario, and Quebec," according to the Center for Aquatic and Invasive Plants (CAIP).

It adds that hydrilla "is present from Florida to Connecticut and west to California and Washington. Its dioecious (separate male and female plants) form is mainly in the southern U.S.; north of South Carolina, hydrilla is mainly monoecious (male and female contained within one plant)."

The two occur together mostly in reservoirs, while hydrilla also thrives in some Florida waterways, such as Toho and Lake Okeechobee, and milfoil competes with native vegetation in northern lakes.

Appearance

Both are submersed, rooted aquatic plants. But there the similarities end. For example, pull a piece of milfoil out of the water on your bait and it will collapse, while hydrilla will remain stiff.

Milfoil features delicate leaflets that give the plant a feathery appearance. Strands can grow as long as 30 feet, but 3 to 10 feet is more typical. When active, the plant is bright green.

Hydrilla leaves occur in whorls of three to eight leaves, but most often five. The midribs of the leaves are reddish in color, with the undersides having small, raised teeth. The stems can grow 20 feet or more.

"Both will top out, but milfoil doesn't create as thick a canopy as hydrilla," said Faircloth, who added that hydrilla often keeps standing longer.

Biology

Both plants prefer stagnant to slowly moving water and can tolerate brackish conditions. In natural lakes, they may crowd out beneficial native vegetation and reducing spawning and feeding habitats. Also, hydrilla is a "mud builder," according to Sam Griffin, a luremaker and former guide on Lake Okeechobee.

When the plant beds die, either from spraying, cold, or overcrowding, they decay into bottom muck that smothers hard bottom spawning areas for bass.

"I don't like hydrilla much," Griffin added. "We caught plenty of fish in the lake before it showed up here in the early 1960s.

But in impoundments that would otherwise offer little habitat, milfoil and hydrilla benefit both bass and bass anglers, even as they cause a myriad of problems for boaters, shoreline property owners, and hydropower plants.

The two plants often will grow in the same areas in these reservoirs, Faircloth said, but hydrilla prefers the edges of breaklines.

"Milfoil will grow right in the middle of a drain, with no distinctive inside or outside edge," he added. "It's patchier with more clumps."

Whether in a reservoir or natural lake, milfoil usually starts growing before hydrilla in the spring, meaning it will be the first to hold fish.

"Bright green, crisp grass will mean more oxygen, more bait, and more bass," Faircloth explained. "Grass that is dead, brown, or decaying is not as healthy and not as good."

As the weather and water warm, hydrilla begins growing faster than milfoil, often crowding it out. As hydrilla reaches the surface, it thickens, intertwines, and mats out to form fish-attracting shade canopies.

On the negative side, if the canopy is too thick, it can kill the plants beneath it by preventing light penetration. When that happens, the infestation results in less oxygen, forcing bass to move, possibly to more hospitable beds of milfoil.

Dead grass on the surface, though, isn't necessarily a bad thing. Plants below it still might be green and holding fish.

But by late summer, "you start seeing the grass (hydrilla) isn't real healthy," the Texas pro said. "And then, as you get into winter, you see it lies over and creates big balls on the bottom contour. A lot of the time, bass will get around and above those balls, instead of under them."

Oddly enough, hydrilla and milfoil can die in spring too, just as they start to grow. "If it comes in fast enough, a big influx of water will kill the grass," he said. "That's because it will stop light penetration. You see that a lot at Rayburn and Toledo Bend."

Strategy

Forced to choose one over the other in a fishery with both aquatic plants, Faircloth would opt for hydrilla. But in reality, seasons and circumstances dictate which aquatic plant he focuses on.

"Growing up on Rayburn, we had both," he said. "In the spring, milfoil can be better because it's the first to grow.

"But milfoil grows straight and keeps standing longer, while hydrilla creates a better canopy."

That canopy provides protection and ambush points for bass, which are edge oriented. Of course, they will be inside hydrilla and milfoil beds as well. But even then, they're more likely to be along the edges of visible holes and pockets, or thinner growth underneath the thicker mats. Not all edges are visible.

Dragging frogs across the top, from hole to hole, is a popular method for taking bass from these mats, as is punching through them with jigs or big worms. Pulling a spinnerbait along the bottom near the outside breakline also can be effective.

For punching, Virginia pro John Crews prefers milfoil beds, which are easier to penetrate and sometimes feature clumps on the outside edges. "I do really well pitching to the clumps," he said.

Faircloth, meanwhile, likes to throw a crankbait or lipless crankbait along the edges and in the openings.

"Hydrilla is thicker and doesn't stick to your bait like milfoil does," he said. "I just use braid to rip the crankbait through. There's no stretch and its clears the bait off better."

He doesn't just look for outside edges either. "On lakes like Rayburn and Toledo Bend, you can have inside edges too," the Texas angler said. "And you can catch fish on both."

To summarize, milfoil starts growing earlier in the spring, meaning it will hold fish sooner. Hydrilla grows faster and can create fish-holding canopies later in the year. But if those canopies grow too thick, they block light, plants die below the surface, and bass might move to more oxygen-rich milfoil beds if they are available. Milfoil usually is easier to "punch" through. For both plants, most of action is likely to be along edges, both inside and out, as well as holes in the beds.

PART TWO: Catching Trophy Bass

The author with smallmouth bass

---

13. The Double-Digit Experience

*J*ust seconds before, I had asked my more experienced partner what to expect if a large bass hits my crankbait. "It will just stop," he said. "And then start to move away."

His final words still hung in the air when the pounding rhythm of the *Jaws* theme wafted across the still water.

"My, God!" I yelled as I set the hook. "That's just what happened!"

Before I felt my citrus Fat Free Shad come to an abrupt halt on that winter afternoon on Mexico's Lake El Salto, I had caught hefty peacock bass, rainbow trout, northern pike, tarpon, snook, sailfish, and a host of other tackle-busting species in waters around the world. But none of them made my heart beat harder and faster than the pot-bellied, pony-eyed pugilist of a game fish that came thrashing to the surface with my crankbait in the corner of her mouth.

This was it! The fish of a lifetime. A 10-pound bass! At least!

Exhibiting incredible strength, this gorgeous monster actually cleared the water twice before I could plunge my rod below the surface in a vain attempt to gain control.

Having none of it, she peeled drag once, twice, three times, ripping out yards of 12-pound-test line. Somehow—probably beginner's luck—I exerted just the right amount of pressure to turn her without pulling so hard I ripped the hook out of her jaw.

Quickly, confidently, and oblivious to my near orgasmic state, the guide pushed the net under the big bass and lifted her out.

Simultaneously, my knees buckled and I collapsed onto the swivel seat. My body was one large tremor as the guide removed the bait and carefully lifted my prize with a hand under her massive belly.

"More than 10," he said. "Maybe 12."

He was right. In fact, she was 12-4.

And for those of you who haven't been as blessed as I was that December day, I can tell you with all sincerity that the experience was just as wonderful as you might imagine.

For a fisherman, especially a freshwater fisherman, nothing beats a 10-pound bass. It's a fish in a million and the fish of a lifetime, and every detail of the epic battle required to subdue it remains etched on your brain in holographic detail for the rest of your life.

Now contrast that double-digit trophy with the 1- to 2-pound bass we're far more likely to catch. The latter isn't an impressive creature by any stretch of the imagination. It's barely bait-size for stripers and tarpon. It wields no swordlike bill and bares no sinister teeth. It sports no flamboyant dorsal fin and flashes no iridescent colors along its flanks. It likely would finish dead last in a race against most other finny predators.

Why, then, do we bother? We bother because we know a 1-pound bass can grow into a 10-pound bass and that at any time, on almost any water in the United States, we could hook into the bass of a lifetime.

But what is it that attracts us to bass in the first place and propels us down the lifelong road toward pursuit of a double-digit?

First, no other sport fish is so available. Although it isn't native to all of them, the largemouth bass now lives in 49 of the 50 states. Only Alaska waters are bass-free. The fact that it has been stocked so abundantly is testament to its popularity.

Also, the largemouth is the most adaptable of game fish. It's not as tolerant of oxygen-poor waters as bullhead or carp, but can thrive in most conditions from shallow lakes and deep reservoirs to turbid rivers and icy streams. It prefers to live as an ambush predator, hiding around cover such as trees, vegetation, and rocks or structure such as humps, points, and ledges. But it can transition to being an open-water hunter when situations dictate.

And this big-mouthed member of the sunfish family is cooperative. Depending on its mood, it will strike just about anything dropped in front of its face. On day as I walked along a lakeshore just before a thunderstorm, I watched bass prowling the shallows. They seemed especially edgy. I tossed a couple of twigs into the water and they struck them aggressively, as if they were the most realistic topwater baits ever created.

This pugnacious nature means kids and even the most inexperienced adults occasionally catch bass by dangling worms for whatever is willing to bite. Looking for greater challenge and excitement, many people become hooked on fishing and gradually replace live bait with artificials. And which sport fish is more available in more waters and more willing to strike than any other?

That's right: Micropterus salmonides, the largemouth bass.

Now factor in the Bass Anglers Sportsman Society, known today as just B.A.S.S. More than 50 years ago they introduced competitive bass fishing, and, in so doing, propelled the black bass—largemouth, smallmouth, and spotted—to an even more prominent role on the angling stage. Competitive fishing spawned innovations in tackle, bass-specific publications such as *Bassmaster Magazine*, and, by logical extension, an even more heightened interest in big bass and how to catch them. Most any freshwater angler today—millions of them—can tell you that the world record largemouth bass weighed 22 pounds, 4 ounces, and most of these folks also know it was caught by George Perry.

Yet that same person probably couldn't tell you the world record weight of any other fish, much less who caught it.

And George Perry just got lucky, many of those same anglers believe. He was an average guy who went fishing on a little lake in Georgia back in 1932, hoping to catch a fish big enough to win a *Field & Stream* fishing contest and feed his family for a couple of days during the Great Depression. He didn't own a big boat or a garage full of fishing tackle. But still he managed to catch the bass that represents the most coveted of all freshwater fishing records.

In other words, if he could do it, so can we. The bass is everyman's fish and the world-record bass is everyman's dream.

Only if you live in Minnesota, Maine, or even Missouri, is this an unrealistic expectation. Theoretically, I suppose, a bass frequenting waters of those states and others in the North and Midwest could grow to more than 20 pounds. In actuality, there's no evidence of it.

But the popularity of bass is such that each individual state's record 13-pounds, 14 ounces in Missouri, for example—is also much coveted. Additionally, a 10-pound largemouth, the gold standard, is possible just about anywhere, although, admittedly, the odds lessen in waters where fish don't grow year around.

And with bass in southern U.S. and Mexico waters routinely surpassing 10 pounds because of mild year-around temperatures and abundant forage, a northern bass angler on a cold winter's night can dream of heading to warmer climes to pursue his double-digit trophy. Pursuing that dream is possible, depending on what he can afford in terms of time and money.

A trip to Florida's Kissimmee Chain, Texas's Lake Fork, or Mexico's Lake El Salto could result in more than just a trophy. Catch a big enough bass and it could make you a millionaire. We don't talk much about that, but we know the way things work in our consumer-driven economy. For the angler who catches a bass that weighs 22 pounds, 5 ounces, every piece of tackle he was using is worth thousands of dollars in endorsements. The fish itself would be worth a considerable amount. And let's not forget the public appearances.

But don't forget either that, for most of us, financial considerations are but a footnote when we go bass fishing. We want to catch a trophy bass because it's the logical culmination of the years of experience we've gained while fishing for bass since we were children. It's confirmation of our prowess in pursuing our nation's most popular game fish. It's a perfect game in bowling, a hole-in-one in golf, a walk-off homerun in the bottom of the ninth of the seventh game of the World Series.

And, best of all, it is attainable. That's the bottom line. A 10-pound fish is a realistic dream for anyone who fishes for bass, and if you are willing to travel to where the monsters live, you could be just a cast away from a world record.

ROBERT MONTGOMERY

---

14. An Accidental Record

*A*nglers sometimes catch what they're *not* fishing for. And sometimes the result is nothing short of mind boggling.

"It still amazes even me," said Barry St. Clair, decades after he caught the Texas state record largemouth bass while fishing for crappie on Lake Fork. That 18.18-pound behemoth fell victim to a 1 ½-inch crappie minnow in about 45 feet of water, on Jan. 24, 1992.

Many mistakenly believe the Texas fisherman caught the big bass on ultralight crappie tackle. That's only partially correct. Having spent the day bass fishing, he and two buddies stopped to catch a few crappie in a deep-water flooded timber, where the papermouth panfish gang up under shad and yellow bass.

Onto his medium-action bass gear with 14-pound line, St. Clair tied on a crappie rig that featured about a foot of 8-pound mono and two 1/0 gold Aberdeen hooks.

"As soon as my bait hit bottom, my rod bent all the way over," he remembered. "I thought it was a big catfish, so I never panicked. I just put pressure on her. I took time to wear the fish out. That helped me get it in, I think."

Once the fish was netted and safely aboard, St. Clair noted the wire hook was in the roof of the fish's mouth and bent at a 30-degree angle. "One more run and she would have been gone," he said.

Since making that improbable catch, the Texas angler said he learned that others have had similar encounters from time to time on Fork. Most of the time, however, the fish win.

"My tackle was stout enough to handle that fish," he said. "Most crappie fishermen aren't using anything nearly strong enough."

But during winter months, lunkers in east Texas timber-filled reservoirs do seem to like the small minnows and jigs offered by crappie anglers.

"Putting the bait in the right place is critical," St. Clair added.

"Big bass hang out with the crappie on timbered flats. They also like bridge pilings that cross creeks. The areas are travel zones and magnets for big fish."

---

15. The Best Big Bass Lake You've Never Heard About

One of the best trophy bass fisheries you've probably never heard of is 2,000-acre Kingsley Lake in northeastern Florida.

How good is it? During 2015, five of the state's ten biggest bass were caught there. Additionally, anglers caught two 15-pound lunkers in one week, including Florida's largest bass of the year, 15-11. Since 2013, the fishery has yielded 90 bass of 10 pounds or more.

Why is it so good? We don't know. But we may soon have a clue because of research being conducted by the Florida Fish and Wildlife Conservation Commission (FWC), with funding assistance from a federal Sport Fish Restoration Program grant.

Kingsley was recognized as an outstanding fishery by Florida's innovative TrophyCatch program, which compiled those impressive numbers based on fishermen who reported their catches of bass weighing 8 pounds or more. The program collects information "through citizen science about trophy bass to help the FWC better enhance, conservative, and promote trophy bass fishing."

FWC tagged and released ten of the TrophyCatch bass, weighing between 9 and 13-pounds, and began monitoring them. The tags contain both temperature and depth sensors to follow fish metabolic rates and movements in this lake that is far deeper than most Florida bass fisheries.

"In reservoirs known for big fish in California and Texas, there are thermal refuges that provide a metabolic advantage," said FWC researcher Drew Dutterer. "Here in Florida, surface water temperatures can reach the upper 90s and even go over 100 degrees on some days.

"When the water is that hot, a bass is that hot as well and its metabolism goes into overdrive, with calories it consumes not going into growth but just to breathe and stay alive."

In contrast to Toho, Kissimmee, Okeechobee and many other Florida lakes, Kingsley has depths of 40 feet or more in at least 300 acres, with a few places that drop below 80. And as of early July, the tagged fish were spending most of their time at 15- to 20-foot depths, where the water temperature was 65 degrees, compared to the upper 80s and low 90s on the surface. Body temperatures of those fish ranged from the upper 70s to the low 80s.

Dutterer added that the fish seem to stay deeper during the day and move shallower at night, but not enough research has been done to determine whether the bass are doing most of their feeding in the shallows.

Based on an examination of stomach contents before those bass were released, biologists believe Kingsley bass primarily eat crappie, bluegill, and redear sunfish. "Big bluegills," the biologist emphasized.

Many Florida fisheries have a more diverse forage base, including shad, chub suckers, and golden shiners, he added. But only shiners have thus far been noted in Kingsley.

Another unique quality of Kingsley is its limited access, with ramps located only at Camp Blanding Joint Training Center.

"There appears to be a process for Kingsley Lake property owners to access the Blanding boat ramps," Dutterer said. "But I believe most boating and fishing is done by current or retired military personnel who can enter the base." But even with restricted access, the biologist added, "it still gets fished pretty hard."

Bass biology, rather than angling pressure, in this rare Florida aquatic environment is what FWC biologists want to better understand.

"We've collected so much data already because of those telemetry tags," Dutterer said. "But it's still too early in the game for us to really know what's going on."

16. The Florida Connection

*I*n southeastern Oklahoma one winter, hatchery ponds for the state's Florida bass stocking program were covered by ice for three weeks. One hundred miles to the south at Lake Fork, just three days were below freezing.

Anglers at Fork during that time probably found the bite tough, but the world-class fishery suffered no long-term damage. In those Oklahoma ponds, 60 percent of the Florida bass brood stock died.

Yes, Florida bass grow faster and larger than their northern counterparts. And stocking them outside their native range has resulted in the creation of some spectacular trophy fisheries in states such as Texas, California, Georgia, and Alabama.

But desired outcome from the expensive effort is not a guarantee.

"In Oklahoma, we finally decided that stocking Florida bass was a waste of time in some places, no matter what fishermen want," said Gene Gilliland, B.A.S.S. National Conservation Director and former assistant chief of fisheries for that state.

Still, anglers continue the drum beat to stock Florida bass in waters biologists say are inappropriate, as Ron Brooks knows all too well. And in their arguments for stocking, they cite "evidence" that really isn't evidence at all, explained the Kentucky fisheries chief.

"We receive requests to stock the Florida strain fairly regularly, and they always site Tennessee's stockings in Kentucky Lake and the larger bass there as a result," he said, echoing the experiences of fisheries managers in several states.

But biologists haven't verified that those large bass are the result of Florida strain stockings. "The truth of the matter is, Kentucky Lake is a fertile lake with very abundant forage species," Brooks added.

Some also wanted Kentucky to stock Florida bass in Cave Run Lake, an infertile fishery east of Lexington, with limited forage and almost no habitat in the lower end. And, oh yeah, muskies—fish that like cold water—do quite well there. Still, Brooks said, explanations for why Cave Run is inappropriate fell on deaf ears.

In a nutshell, here's what introduced Florida bass need to thrive: a mild climate, abundant forage, and plentiful habitat, preferably vegetation. Originating in subtropic Florida, they're most at home in shallow water with a long growing season and plenty to eat.

For survival, climate is the most critical of the three. A temperature drop of a few degrees can stress Florida bass, and a rapid and/or severe drop may kill them. Unfortunately, a clear geographic boundary for determining where Florida bass can live and where they can't does not exist.

"It's not a north/south thing," Gilliland said. "It's a diagonal, with cold moving from the northwest to the southeast."

To thrive, Florida bass require plenty of food both throughout the year and during all stages of their life cycle. In their native range that means mostly golden shiners, shad, and sunfish. But they will grow large and fat on other species, including trout in California and tilapia in Mexico's Lake El Salto.

Shallow-water, vegetated habitat is the least critical of the three components, especially if the climate is mild and food plentiful.

Okay, some of you say, "I understand that. But what's the big deal if you stock Florida bass in a lake and they don't do well. No harm, no foul. Right?"

Wrong.

Introducing Florida bass is not the same as a supplemental stocking to enhance a depleted fishery. There's only one reason to stock them: To grow trophy fish. If a water body isn't conducive for that, then Florida genes mixed into the native strain may actually harm the fishery, making them less hardy, at least in the short term. Eventually the Florida genes will disappear from the population.

But the money wasted to maintain brood stock, spawn them, and stock the offspring will have been wasted.

Additionally, as Florida bass breed with native bass, the potential for growing to trophy size is lost over time. "You can't just stock and leave them," Gilliland said. "As long as you have 50 percent or greater Florida genes, there's still potential. Below that, it's no greater than with just native fish."

Still, many anglers who want big bass in their home waters continue lobbying for something that isn't in the best interests of their fisheries.

"Believe me, if past research projects indicated Florida strain bass would produce lunker bass in Kentucky, we would have stocked them years ago," said Brooks, voicing the frustration of many fisheries managers. "We strive to produce the best fisheries possible within the limits of our resources."

Meanwhile, in Tennessee . . .

Can Tennessee biologists turn Chickamauga into another Lake Fork?

Probably not.

That Texas lake is the gold standard for trophy bass fisheries, and duplicating the success there isn't a reasonable expectation, especially for a state with a less hospitable climate.

But resource managers are hopeful they can grow bigger bass in Chickamauga through the introduction of Florida-strain largemouths into the population.

"I'm convinced that Florida bass will grow big in Tennessee," said Bobby Wilson, fisheries chief for the Department of Wildlife Resources (DWR). "I hope that can happen in Chickamauga. And if it does we'll move to other lakes with it."

So far, Wilson has two persuasive pieces of evidence to support his conviction: In October of 2009, biologists electroshocked a 16-15 largemouth at Browns Creek Lake, where Florida bass also have been stocked. And in February of 2015, Gabe Keen caught a state record at Chickamauga that tipped the scales at 15.2 pounds. The previous record, caught in 1954, weighed 14 pounds, 8 ounces (14.5).

"We've had a few 13-pounders reported by fishermen (from agency lakes)," Wilson added. "They were probably Florida bass."

Still, the overall verdict remains out on Chickamauga.

The same goes for Lake Guntersville, just to the south in Alabama.

"We haven't stocked them (Florida bass) on a regular basis," said Keith Floyd of the Alabama Department of Conservation. "It's been periodically in one or two embayments, to see if we can incorporate Florida genomes into the population."

Tennessee, however, has been much more deliberate in its approach. After stocking 200,000 fry annually for five years throughout Chickamauga failed to show much of a genetic shift, biologists decided to focus on three creeks for the next five years.

"Anglers (at Chickamauga) say they're catching bigger bass," Wilson explained. "And they say the bass look different from what they're used to seeing."

Anglers also are catching bigger bass at Lake Atkins in adjacent Arkansas, where the fishery was rehabilitated and then stocked with Florida bass. In 2011, anglers caught at least three 12-pound bass in that 752-acre fishery.

Wilson said his state used criteria from Arkansas and Oklahoma in deciding where Florida-strain bass could be stocked successfully in Tennessee. That turned out to be south of a line from Dyersburg in the west to Chattanooga in the east.

But as Virginia proved during the early 1990s, bass with Florida genes can do well even farther north than that. After being stocked in the late 1980s, Briery Creek Lake yielded a 13-4 trophy in 1992. It followed with a 16-3 (one ounce shy of the state record) in 1995 and 16-2 in 2002. And from 1994 to 2002, it produced the largest bass in the state annually.

"A lot of people are excited about this," Wilson said about Tennessee's Florida bass program. "But some don't want them because they've heard they're more finicky than northern bass."

And there's the argument that native bass populations are weakened by adding Florida bass. "But these aren't native systems," the Tennessee fisheries chief pointed out. "These are manmade impoundments."

Texas' long-term success with Florida bass in Lake Fork and other reservoirs provides a strong argument in support of Wilson. And the fact that more than 500 largemouth bass of 13 pounds and more have been entered in its ShareLunker program seems to dispel the "finicky" fear as well.

Personal experience

From my own decades of fishing for Florida bass in Florida, Texas, and Mexico, I've noted that Florida bass can turn off when temperature drops just a degree or two. But I don't find them more difficult to catch than northern bass. When cold and/or high pressure turns them off, you just have to slow down and adjust your tactics. Instead of throwing a spinnerbait, flip a soft plastic along the edge of a weedline.

Also, I've found Florida bass to be, pound for pound, much more challenging fighters than northern bass. A big Florida is like a mean smallmouth with a belly. And I've seen 12-pounders tail walk.

Count me as one who isn't troubled by the occasional finickiness of Florida bass or the fact that they're being introduced into manmade fisheries in Tennessee, Arkansas, Alabama, and perhaps other states outside their native range. I've been blessed to catch a few double-digit Florida bass, and I'd like to see more opportunities for other anglers to do so as well.

Whether Chickamauga and Guntersville are two of the fisheries capable of consistently growing those genetically enhanced big fish will probably be revealed in the years ahead.

17. Pickwick Giant

*M*ost of the time, the "big one" gets away.

When it doesn't, an angler can confront an ethical dilemma: Should he do what's necessary to get his catch certified, risking its death? Or should he quickly measure and photograph the fish before releasing it to live on and possibly be caught again.

Lance Walker chose the latter option while fishing Pickwick Lake in January 2011 with Ray Rittenhour, a deacon from his church. Using a Yumbrella umbrella rig (with only three baits), he caught and released what could have been a record largemouth for Tennessee waters rather than risk its life to officially establish a new record.

Since surpassed on Chickamauga Lake, the record at the time was a 14.5-largemouth caught by James Barnett on Sugar Creek in 1954. Walker was praised for his actions by many and criticized by a few people who either doubt his sanity or question the size of the bass.

Walker can live with that. "The debate will always go on. If someone wants to say the fish weighed 10 pounds, that's fine," he said.

"I caught a 13.3 (on Pickwick) that was certified and this one could have swallowed her. I'm not claiming to have the state record. I just caught a big fish. But I know the state record lives on Pickwick Lake."

Jimmy Mason, a guide and professional angler, has no doubt Walker is telling the truth about the size of his fish. "I would stake my reputation on his credibility," he said. "And there are few people I'd do that with. Lance isn't looking to get any notoriety from this."

But both Walker and Mason, who caught a 10.7 largemouth while fishing with his friend on Pickwick a few days later, would like this Tennessee River fishery to receive more publicity. Mason believes Pickwick is a better big-bass fishery than Guntersville, and Walker's catch certainly helps with that argument. The Guntersville Lake record is 14.5, according to the Alabama Department of Conservation and Natural Resources.

Meanwhile, the Pickwick bass that was released weighed . . . well, we really don't know. But here's what we do know:

The fish bottomed out Walker's 15-pound scales. At Pickwick Landing State Park it weighed 14.58 pounds on another angler's scales.

With plenty of witnesses around to watch, the fish was measured at 27 1/8 inches long and 24 inches around. Plugging those figures into various weight calculators, Walker said, placed the weight between 14.5 and 15.7, "with the consensus being around 14.8."

Using an International Game Fish Association length/girth formula for calculating weight, the fish would have weighed 16.7 pounds. And World Fishing Network cited that another calculation put the weight at about 16.5.

Based on what his eyes told him, Walker believes the bass weighed at least 15 pounds and possibly 16. If that's not incredible enough, he thinks the fish was pure Northern strain.

Had he taken the bass away from the Pickwick for a certifying weight with two witnesses, biologists with the Tennessee Wildlife Resources Agency understandably would have wanted to check its genetics.

"Needless to say, the fish had to die in order to do this, it seemed to me and Ray," said Walker. "There was never any thought process for me that the fish would leave the lake." So Walker, his son Cole, and Rittenhour took the potential state record back out into Pickwick and released her.

"Let me tell you, she tore out of my hand and was unharmed," Walker said. He understands the need for certifying record catches, but adamantly insisted "there's no reason to kill a fish like that."

In hindsight, he realizes he might have been able to get the fish certified without blood sample and fin clip being taken, but added, "I was an emotional wreck from catching her."

He would like to see certified scales available at Pickwick Landing as well as other locations around the lake. That's more important than ever, he believes, because the lake has turned into a big-fish factory. Not long after Walker's catch someone called to tell him about a 12-plus taken on Pickwick. And on a Sunday afternoon in January, Walker's son caught an 8 and a 7 on back-to-back casts with the Yumbrella rig.

"The lake is healthy with lots of shad and clearly the grass has helped. It gave a jumpstart to everything," he said.

Mason added, "Pickwick has just exploded in both quantity and quality. Once we started getting grass in the lake, it just took off."

Part of the equation, too, could be that the umbrella rig and its variations are tapping into populations of big bass that have gone largely untouched in fisheries throughout the country. These fish suspend around schools of shad, particularly during cooler weather, and when anglers find the forage, they drop down their multi-lure offerings to the eager bass.

But whatever the reason, Walker believes his catch was a "blessing from God" and that releasing her uncertified was the right thing to do.

18. Recognition Programs

*T*rophyCatch was exceeding expectations five years after it began in 2012, according to Tom Champeau, fisheries chief for the Florida Fish and Wildlife Conservation Commission (FWC).

"We're happy with the how the program has grown," he added. "We've had more than 6,000 submissions. And that provides us with a lot of insights as to where big fish are in Florida, when they're caught, and the frequency with which they're caught. It really helps us (for managing fisheries)."

TrophyCatch is a citizen-science conservation reward program for bass anglers that emphasizes live-release of largemouth bass weighing eight pounds and heavier. During the first five years, 47 bass weighing 13 pounds or more were reported, with the largest checking in at 16-12.

It was caught in a "neighborhood pond" on March 18, 2017.

One of the biggest surprises to come out of TrophyCatch has been the number of trophy bass taken in residential retention and golf course ponds, Champeau said.

"These ponds are everywhere in Florida and we can look at how they're managed," he added. "They tell us the big fish are out there and that even people fishing from the bank can catch them."

Kingsley Lake, a 2,000-acre semi-private fishery in the northeastern part of the state, also yielded unexpected productivity. Hundreds of bass weighing 8 pounds or more were caught there, including 13 weighing 13 pounds or more and two that topped 15 pounds.

"Kingsley is a sinkhole lake and we have others like that," the fisheries chief said.

On the flip side, Lake Kissimmee and the Kissimmee Chain, with more than 100,000 acres of public water, topped public waters for entries. "We predicted that," Champeau said.

Likely of most interest to anglers, data from five years of TrophyCatch combined with information from a trophy bass tagging program allowed FWC to extrapolate that anglers annually catch between 2,500 and 4,500 bass weighing 8 pounds or more, from a statewide pool of 15,000 to 30,000 trophy fish.

"Those are all the big bass we know about (reported via TrophyCatch) and those we don't know about," said FWC researcher Drew Dutterer. "Those statistics have been consistent across five years."

He added, "Trophy bass are a pretty big priority for our agency and the state of Florida. It's one of the identifying characteristics of our Florida bass fishery, and one reason a lot of people come during the winter and take fishing vacations in Florida is the chance to catch a big fish."

Champeau is also pleased that TrophyCatch has helped promote freshwater fishing in general and especially conservation and catch-and-release. "A lot of fish were returned that might otherwise have been mounted," he said. "It (TrophyCatch) has been a great tool for teaching anglers how to handle fish. We encourage immediate release and improved survival."

Finally, TrophyCatch also helped FWC build partnerships with the fishing industry, the media, and manufacturers as sponsors of the program. "Hopefully, they've seen the benefits too, both for conservation and their businesses," Champeau said.

The beginning

In 1986, the first largemouth bass entered in Texas' fledgling ShareLunker program also proved to be a state record, weighing 17.67 pounds.

Since then, anglers fishing Texas waters have caught nearly 600 bass weighing at least 13 pounds, including more than 50 that weighed 15 pounds or better. Among them is, an 18.18 record caught in 1992.

It's almost a certainty all of those fish were either Florida-strain largemouths or carried Florida genes that enabled their trophy stature. Coincidentally, Florida's state record, weighing 17.27 pounds, was also taken in 1986.

During that same time anglers fishing Florida waters have caught . . . Well, we don't know how many trophy largemouths they caught. Texas took the lead in recording and promoting Florida bass in its waters. But the state for which they're named? Not so much.

That changed with TrophyCatch, starting in October 2012.

"We do mirror the ShareLunker program in some ways," said Champeau. "A lot of anglers liked the ShareLunker program so we sent some of our staff to Texas to see what they were doing."

A key difference, though, is that the Lone Star State uses the big bass in its hatcheries to create even more lunkers for its reservoirs. Florida bass are not native to Texas. By contrast, many of the Sunshine State's lakes, ponds, and rivers are naturally populated by Florida strain bass. In other words, breeding stock isn't needed.

A golf course lake, a retention pond, a canal—just about any body of water in Florida could be home to a state-record bass just waiting to be caught—and entered into TrophyCatch.

As a matter of fact, in this state the Florida bass calls home, dozens of fish of state-record proportion—and possibly even a world record or two—have been caught but were not verified by FWC personnel. At RiverBassin.com, you can see a list of "unofficial" big bass, including several of more than 20 pounds and more than two dozen heavier than the current record.

Appropriately, then, FWC states proudly on the TrophyCatch website that "no other place on earth has this largemouth bass promotion opportunity."

If bass aren't needed for reproduction, what is the value of offering incentives to anglers who catch, document, and report their catches of bass weighing 8 pounds or more? Genetic research certainly, to find out more about the unique strain of bass that soon might by reclassified from a subspecies to a separate species of black bass. But also to "promote and celebrate our fisheries," said Champeau.

"We want to promote fishing, catch and release, and environmental stewardship to keep our fisheries healthy," he explains.

That's one of four cornerstones upon which TrophyCatch was created as the "promotional engine" for the state's Black Bass Management Plan. Use of sound science, public involvement in management of the resource, and adaptive management are the other three. Adaptive management involves constant monitoring and periodic adjustment to reach an end point, as opposed to inflexible policies.

ShareLunker

Starting in 2018, more anglers became eligible to participate in Texas' Toyota ShareLunker program, as Texas Parks and Wildlife (TPW) announced big changes in the strategy designed to grow bigger bass for the state's fisheries.

First, the program that began in 1986 is now year-around instead of beginning in the fall and ending in spring. Most importantly, bass weighing 8 pounds and more now are eligible, a qualification identical to Florida's TrophyCatch.

"Angler recognition continues to be a primary goal of the Toyota ShareLunker program," said Kyle Brookshear, program coordinator.

"This year, for the first time ever, anglers who catch a largemouth bass 8 pounds or larger can participate simply by providing important catch information we can use to improve bass fisheries science.

"We will be recognizing and rewarding these anglers as well as those anglers who loan their lunker bass weighing 13 pound or greater to our breeding program during the spawning season."

ShareLunker now has four levels: Lunker Legacy Class, Lunker Legend Class, Lunker Elite Class, and Lunker Class.

Lunker Legacy is awarded to anglers who loan bass of 13 pounds or larger during the spawning period from Jan. 1 to March 31

"These valuable fish are an integral piece of the Toyota ShareLunker selective breeding and stocking program and anglers will be eligible for an exciting prize package commensurate with the importance of sharing their lunker," TPW said.

Lunker Legend will apply to those who enter a largemouth bass of 13 pounds or more from Jan. 1 to Dec. 31, while Lunker Elite is for anglers catching a bass weighing from 10 to 12.99 pounds. Anglers who enter a bass of at least 8 pounds or 24 inches in length from Jan. 1 to Dec. 31 will earn Lunker Class recognition.

All qualifiers in the latter three will receive a Toyota ShareLunker Catch Kit, containing branded merchandise, fishing tackle, an achievement decal, and entry into the year-end ShareLunker prize drawing for a $5,000 shopping spree and an annual fishing license.

Anglers who catch qualifying fish can enter them using a ShareLunker mobile application with their smartphones. It is free to download on iTunes and Google Play, as well as on the new ShareLunker website. Digital entry forms allow anglers to submit photos of their fish being measured, weighed, and held. Additionally, anglers will be able to provide genetic samples of their fish by collecting and sending scales to TPW using instructions from the application and website.

"Monitoring the impact of ShareLunker stockings is critical to evaluating the success of the program," Brookshear said. "That's why the citizen scientist piece is so important.

"We need anglers to help us better understand the populations of our biggest bass in Texas and we're excited to offer exciting prizes in exchange for providing us with the information and genetic material from their lunker catches."

Hatcheries staff will attempt to spawn all eligible ShareLunkers 13 pounds or larger donated between Jan. 1 and March 31. Offspring of female genetic intergrades will be combined and stocked in the source locations for all ShareLunker entries for the year. Meanwhile, genetically pure offspring will be maintained at the Texas Freshwater Fisheries Center and eventually distributed to all TPWD production hatcheries as brood stock for statewide largemouth bass stockings.

"Our goal is for all hatchery-held Florida largemouth bass brood stock to eventually be the descendants of ShareLunkers," Brookshear said. "Increasing the percentage of ShareLunker offspring being introduced into Texas waters is an important part of increasing the lunker genetic potential in the state.

"We are incredibly grateful for anglers who choose to loan us these valuable fish and we look forward to continuing our efforts to make Texas fishing bigger and better with the selective breeding program."

19. A Classic Story

*A*uthor's note: Years ago, fishing legend Bill Dance told me about the two most memorable bass he ever lost. One of them involved a smallmouth bass of staggering proportions, a trophy fish in the truest sense. I detailed that battle on Pickwick Lake in *Why We Fish*. The other bass was considerably smaller, but a "trophy" nevertheless. Bill's encounter with this unforgettable fish occurred during the 1973 Bassmaster Classic at Clark Hill Reservoir on the South Carolina/Georgia border. In Bill's own words, here's the story:

* * * * *

I had a school of bass that ranged from 38 to 52 feet deep. It was a deep pattern, where a creek channel met the Savannah River. A long point went out and plummeted off. At the end it was 52 feet, dropping into the creek and river.

I caught a limit every day there. Back then, you could weigh in ten fish. I think I might have been the only one to catch a limit every day. But Rayo Breckenridge won that tournament. He beat me by 2 ½ to 3 pounds.

You could only take ten pounds of tackle to the tournament. I had ten Bill Jackson Super Floaters, which were purple worms with white polka dots all over them, 6 inches long. I Carolina-rigged them.

Searcy (Charles, the outdoor writer for the *Nashville Tennessean* at the time) said he knew he couldn't offer me advice or help me catch a fish in any way, but he said he could feed me. So he stuck a Butterfinger in my mouth as I fished.

A film crew recorded the action. They pulled up to me and I had a bass on about 5 ½ pounds. It came out of 40 to 45 feet of water. I fought him up and he didn't fight very much. He was a lot of weight, but just a little tug.

That film crew was sitting out from me about 25 to 30 feet. As the fish came to the top, it rolled and jumped. I don't think the fish even knew he was hooked. He was real docile. Just before I could grab him, someone on the film crew said, "Wait a minute. Let him come back around."

My hand was right there. I definitely could have grabbed that fish. But, like an idiot, I let the fish go back out. The fish made a little surge. Then he jumped a second time and threw the worm.

They (film crew) said the fish weighed 8 pounds. It didn't. It weighed 4 ½ to 5 pounds. It was a good fish. I would have won the tournament if I had jerked that fish in the boat.

That fish will always be a memorable fish. I was so depressed. But I was proud for Rayo.

My wife called me off to the side. I was real, real disappointed. Disappointed in myself and disappointed that I didn't win Classic. She said, "Look at me. Everything in life happens for a reason. There's a reason you didn't win. There's a reason Rayo did."

She said the Good Lord favored Rayo this time. His wife was going blind and needed money for an operation. Marilyn had talked to Diane about that. That win would really help them out financially. Me losing gave someone sight for the rest of her life. I'll never forget that. Everything happens for a reason. I told myself, "She's right."

It made me feel 100 percent better. I'd do it again if I knew it would help someone mentally or physically.

It happened on the last day. That will always be a memorable lost fish, but the fact that it did a lot of good makes me feel a whole lot better.

Rayo was a modest guy; a credit to our sport and a true Southern gentleman.

Life has lot of happy moments and a plenty of disappointments. Everything happens for a reason. Those were great days back then. It's not about the pounds or numbers of fish you caught. You can weigh those. But they don't even come close to the memories. Our memories outweigh all of that—the good times, fun times, and sad times. They were all part of it. It's been a good ride.

ROBERT MONTGOMERY

20. What I Learned in Canada

*A*lthough I love catching bass, I'm not a purist. I'm happy to engage with any fish that takes my bait. That's a major reason I enjoy fishing in Canada and our northern tier of states. Walleye, muskie, and northern pike will attack bass offerings. Heck, I even caught an Atlantic salmon while fishing for smallmouths in New Brunswick.

But the aforementioned toothy critters are the most likely incidental catches. I also caught a 20-pound-plus northern on a Senko and another on a jig, as well as a 16-pound muskie on a lipless crankbait. Of course I've also come in second best more than a few times because monofilament and fluorocarbon don't hold up well against sharp teeth. I'll never forget the massive muskie that came out from under our boat and engulfed my Rat-L-Trap just as I was about to lift it out of the water. It sliced the line with surgical precision and was gone—with my bait—in the blink of an eye.

Of course if you've a purist and don't want muskie and northern interfering with your bass fishing, all you have to do is use a wire leader. You won't catch many bass, but you won't lose baits. Based on my own experience, you probably won't catch northern or muskie either. They seem to strike only when you're *not* using wire.

I also like fishing up north because of the long daylight hours during summer. Depending on where you are and the month, twilight might not arrive until 10 o'clock or even midnight.

Bugs top of the list of things I don't like. You think mosquitoes are bad in the Everglades or Louisiana swamps? Well . . . they are. But they're just as numerous and relentless on northern waters—and they grow larger than their southern counterparts. You can make a cast and be down a pint before you get your bait back. Additionally, the hordes of black flies and no-see-ums (biting midges) are ferocious. You're subject to attack at any time during summer, but June usually is the worst month. I've also learned to take a head net.

Here's what else I learned in Canada:

1. Retie regularly, even though you don't think you need to, and especially if you're catching fish.

I'll never forget watching a huge smallie swim away with my white spinnerbait in his mouth. It could have been the largest I've ever hooked but I'll never know because I got lazy. I had boated a couple of dozen hard-fighting bass previous to that, using just 10-pound line because of the clear water. And, as I caught fish after fish, the knot progressively weakened until that critical moment when the largest bass of the day took the bait, fought hard, and the knot parted just as I was about to lip my trophy.

2. Smallmouth bass put on a heavy slime coating to help them survive the winters.

At least that's what a guide in New Brunswick told me after I boated one that appeared to be covered in snot. I was concerned the fish was sick or diseased. He assured me the yucky stuff dripping off the bronzeback was normal. All things considered, I believe I'd prefer a down vest.

3. We're lucky smallmouth bass don't grow larger and have teeth.

We flew into the Ontario bush and then trekked to a small lake my guide told me was rarely, if ever fished. The fish acted like it, too. We caught them on every cast. After that got boring I reeled my jig up to the end of my rod and then just swirled it around in the water near the boat. And I still caught bass!

Seeing such aggression actually made me a little fearful of falling in the water. If I had, it would have been death by a million bites, not a thousand. Sadly, most of the fish we caught were between 8 and 10 inches, suggesting the lake had way too many predators for the forage base.

4. I'd go fishing in Canada just for the shore lunches.

Fresh-caught walleye fried to perfection is hard to beat, and no one does it better than guides in Canada. But I'll pass on those sandwiches that feature butter on one slice of bread and mayonnaise on the other.

5. Contrary to what many anglers believe, the black bass is not a universally loved fish.

In New Brunswick, fishermen used to shake their heads in disgust when they caught smallmouths, before tossing them onto the shore to die. That's because they wanted to catch native salmon and trout, and bass were illegally introduced invaders. Popularity of the bass has improved considerably during the past few decades, but some who fish northern waters, where it is not native, still don't like it.

6. Don't get caught in the Canadian bush after dark. And I'm not talking about a threat posed by bears or wolves.

After a day's fishing on a remote lake in New Brunswick, several of us relaxed on the screened porch of a cabin where we were spending the night. As dusk turned into night, I noted a slight whining sound in the woods around us.

Quickly it intensified and grew closer. In seconds, it was right there, just a few feet from us, so loud that we almost couldn't hear one another speak. Screens in the door and windows actually vibrated under the mosquito assault.

And I prayed I wouldn't need to visit the outhouse that night.

PART THREE: Think Like a Bass: Biology and Behavior

The author with a crankbait bass

21. Bass Suck

We say that bass bite. But really they suck.

They suck soft plastics, jigs, spinnerbaits, crankbaits, and, yes, occasionally even topwaters. When a lure disappears into a subtle dimple on the surface, it was sucked in by a fish directly below it.

Suction feeding isn't the only way bass take forage or bait, but it's likely the most common. Ram feeding is the other primary method. In this case, the bass moves forward with its mouth open, engulfing prey. Depending on conditions and the fish's aggressiveness, these can be employed separately or in combination. Understanding the mechanics of these behaviors can make you a better angler.

Bass employ these strategies "because they don't have thumbs," said Gene Gilliland, B.A.S.S. National Conservation Director and a long-time fisheries biologist in Oklahoma.

Nor do they have claws, teeth, or hooked beaks to capture, bite, and tear. If bass and other predatory fish species were air-breathing animals, they would probably starve to death. But water is their element, and they are perfectly adapted for that liquid environment.

"It's all part of fluid dynamics," said Gilliland, explaining suction feeding. "When a bass opens its mouth, it creates a vacuum that pulls in water—and prey. The density of the prey isn't too much different than the water.

"And it happens so fast."

In fact, video documentation shows a bass needs just 1/24 of a second to suck in prey. And the same amount of time to spit it out again.

That "tick, tick" you sometimes feel, prompting you to set the hook only to discover you missed the fish? That might be what happened.

"How can a bass suck in a bait with three sets of trebles and not get hooked?" said the conservation director, posing a question countless anglers have asked themselves over the years while shaking their heads in disbelief.

The bait is surrounded by water, not air, and the water acts as a buffer around it, allowing the bass to spit it out. But if the bass like what it feels and decides to eat the fish or bait, then it clamps down and expels the water through its gills.

In ram feeding a bass opens its mouth as it swims behind its prey, trying to overtake and consume it. The problem is, movement toward the bait creates a bow wave, actually pushing away what it's trying to catch. That's why suction is often utilized as well.

"It's hard to move water (with suction)," Gilliland said. "It takes a lot of muscle power to create that force and the muscles in the head aren't enough to do that. A bass employs muscles all the way down its body."

He also pointed out that predators are typically faster than prey and forage fish can't see behind them, both advantages for bass.

With a surface bite, air is frequently engulfed with water and the bait, especially if the strike is explosive. That means there's not as much of a water cushion to separate trebles from flesh, increasing the angler's odds of a hookup if he can manage to wait a split-second for the fish to turn and dive. But if the bait is subtly sucked down, usually the hookset must be rapid, before the bass spits it out. In fact, if an angler isn't watching his lure, he might not even know a bass had it.

Likewise, underwater video reveals that bass often suck in and spit out soft plastics, jigs, and even crankbaits without anglers on the other end of those baits feeling a thing. That's why a sensitive rod tip is important in so many applications.

To a lesser extent, bass employ a third type of feeding, also utilized by striped bass, tuna, and other predators. With their mouths closed they will hit prey to stun or kill it, before sucking it in. They most often do this when pursuing schools of shad, alewives, or herring in open water. Those who shiner fish for bass often observe this behavior.

On the other hand, panfish and even smaller bass usually are captured by ambush, meaning use of suction or a combination of suction/ram feeding. Either way, if a bass grabs a large spiny-finned entree from behind, it can get a mouthful in more ways than one. Many mistakenly assume the fish simply manipulates the forage so it can swallow it head first and compress the dorsal spines.

But again, as Gilliland said, bass "don't have thumbs."

"When a bass inhales and the bluegill isn't positioned right, if it's too large, it can get stuck and there's not a lot a bass can do to dislodge it," he said. "If it gets stuck, then breathing is inhibited, the mouth is locked open, and the bass suffocates.

"A bass might take a fish head first or tail first," he added. "The point is that it takes a fish whichever way it can."

That probably explains why bass in controlled feeding studies selected forage toward the center of the size range, as opposed to larger offerings, according to Hal Schramm, a fisheries researcher at Mississippi State University.

"How big a forage fish can bass eat?" he added. "Largemouth can easily swallow a forage fish up to one-third its length. A smallmouth can slurp up a forage fish that's one-fourth its length."

Another way of judging what a bass can eat comes from a study by the Florida Fish and Wildlife Conservation Commission. It concluded, "Any prey having a body depth less than the diameter of the bass' mouth may be consumed. A bass will grasp its food any way it can, but usually tries to swallow fish head first."

But when Gilliland worked as a fisheries biologist in Oklahoma, "We took bluegill and crappie out (of bass) that, we thought, no way a bass could have swallowed," he recalled.

One crappie in the stomach of a 3-pound bass had a 5-inch depth.

"There's no way that bass' mouth was 5 inches," the conservation director said. "But I guess it's like a snake eating a rabbit. There's a lot of stretching going on.

"Bass are opportunistic feeders. They eat first and ask questions later."

---

22. Night Sight

*F*or many night fishermen, any worm color will work—as long as it's red.

But based on what we know about bass vision and the properties of light and color in water, those night-feeding fish probably can't see red, especially in deeper water.

"I don't know what the bass are keying on, but I can guarantee you they aren't seeing red," said Dr. Hal Schramm, a professor and fisheries leader at the Mississippi Cooperative Fish & Wildlife Unit and an avid angler.

"You need only listen to a few tournament speeches to realize that even some pro anglers have serious misconceptions about bass vision," added Dr. Keith Jones, longtime director of research at the Berkley Fish Research Center in Spirit Lake, Iowa, and the author of *Knowing Bass*.

"What they believe the bass sees and what the bass actually sees are often miles apart."

Still, there's a reason bass hit red worms after dark, and it likely relates to vision. Better understanding how and what bass see in their underwater world, both day and night, can help you bring more fish to the boat.

First, why aren't those night-feeding bass seeing red?

Visible light consists of a spectrum of wave lengths from red to violet. As the shortest of those, red light penetrates the least, while green goes deeper, and blue deeper still. For example, red light goes to just 6 feet in clear water, with yellow to 19, green to 30, and blue to almost 40, Schramm said. In "moderately clear water," their visibility is 1.5, 5, 7.5, and 10 feet respectively.

In other words, if you're fishing a red worm, no matter the time of day, if you're going much below 6 feet, bass aren't seeing that bait as red.

Now factor in the fish's visual limitations.

"Their eyes adjust gradually to the dark, just like ours do, and I think they have better vision than we give them credit for," said Stephen Headrick, a veteran night angler and owner of Punisher Lures on Dale Hollow Lake. "But you don't hear fish feeding (on top) during the dark of the moon or when it's halfway. That's because they relate to the bottom more because they can't see as well."

Jones added that the eyes of people and fish contain the same basic components and serve the same function, "which is to gather and organize light, and then convert it to a nerve signal." But, he cautioned, anglers shouldn't mistakenly believe bass see what we see when we go underwater with a face mask.

By day, better depth perception and the ability to see a broader range of motions and images enhances vision for bass.

"In the daytime, when vision is dominated by cone cells, bass have enough light to appreciate subtle variations in motion, fine details, and color," Jones said. "They can thoroughly critique a lure because they have more visual information to work with. Consequently, the angler's choice of lure size, shape, action, and color pattern may all prove critical, since they can all be easily seen."

At night, though, rod cells take over for vision in low light. They're more sensitive than cone cells, but less helpful for color, depth perception, contrasting objects, and resolving details.

"For a bass out searching for a nighttime meal, the finer points of prey quality take a back seat to simply finding the prey," Jones explained.

Fish do that by contrasting their prey against something lighter or darker. In doing so, they see the shape, but not the detail. That's why topwaters sometimes are a good choice, and it's why black and darker shades of brown, purple, and, yes, red, are good choices for night fishing. Also, color contrasts on the baits themselves, such as chartreuse or orange on plastics and jigs, or gold blades on spinnerbaits can help get the attention of bass.

"On a dark night, you want a dark color, especially in warm water," said Headrick, who added that another productive tactic can be matching your bait's color to that of crawfish that bass, especially smallmouths, are eating.

"Crawfish spawn every 30 days starting at 55 degrees," he explained. 'When the water is cold, the crawfish is light. If it's hot, then it's a dark color. And it turns green when it's spawning.

"A yellow jig works well in winter because crawfish are a light color."

Whether an angler offers a yellow jig or a dark red worm, his chances of getting the attention of his quarry is enhanced by a bass's field of vision, whether night or day.

"Fish have a field of vision that would make the best hunter jealous," Schramm said.

On a bass, each protruding eye on the side of its head views at an almost complete 180-degree arc that extends from behind the fish to past the mid-point in front, including top and bottom as well.

Blind spots are limited to directly behind, because of obstruction by the gill plates and stomach, as well as directly below and, to a lesser extent, above.

Night stalkers

While bass use all their senses to forage at night, anglers benefit from technology to catch those feeding fish. "People used to fish at night to get away from the heat and the boat traffic," said Stephen Headrick, owner of Punisher Lures. "But now there's a third reason: Great electronics."

Of course that means GPS and sonar for "seeing" below the water, but it also includes accessories for improving angler vision after dark.

One of those is Headrick's Cast & Glo Super Light, which improves dramatically on the ultraviolet lights anglers have used for decades to highlight fluorescent line and help them see bites. In addition to an 8-LED white light for inside the boat, it features two rows of 24-LED lights that can be used as standard black lights. But the top row can also be switched to green.

"I leave the green light on all the time," Headrick said. "It doesn't bother the fish and it lights up everything."

He came up with the idea, he explained, because anglers were asking for green lights to use during night tournaments. Previously they relied on light sticks in clear containers, which they used to illuminate the outside edges of grass beds. But dropping those sticks also aided their competitors.

"Now they just use my light," the Tennessee luremaker said. "Guys in Alabama, Georgia, and northern Louisiana love it."

Other senses

Day or night, a bass is primarily a sight feeder. But other senses also play vital roles in helping it track down forage, especially in darkness. For example, water is much denser than air so sound travels farther and faster in it. That means a bass might be alerted to an approaching shad school by what it hears instead of what it sees.

"Most fish have an adequate sense of vision, but this is usually not so impressive as their sense of smell and ability to detect vibrations through their lateral lines," added Dr. David Ross, a scientists emeritus at Woods Hole Oceanographic Institution.

"Fish usually use their sense of hearing or smell to initially perceive their prey, and then use their vision only in the final attack."

The lateral line is a series of pores or canals in a row of scales that stretch from behind the gill plate to nearly the tail. This extraordinary adaption allows bass to do more than simply hear other fish. The line detects vibrations and sends a signal to the brain, which interprets them as a sound that directs the bass to its origin.

Night bites

- Research suggests the eyes of a bass continue to grow throughout the lifespan. Bigger eyes with better vision could be one reason that trophy bass are more difficult to fool with artificial baits.

- No, bass don't have eyelids. But their eyes do have a black pigment that allows them to see in bright light without discomfort. Likely they prefer to stay in shade to use the dark-light contrast as an ambush advantage. That way they can see their prey more easily than the prey can see them.

- A primary reason bass don't grow to trophy size in turbid or dingy water is because they can't see well enough to find adequate prey.
- Our eyes adjust faster to dark than do those of bass. That's possibly why the bite is sometimes slower during the first two hours of darkness and last two hours before daylight.
- Some historians believe pirates wore patches not because of battle injuries, but to preserve night vision. They frequently had to move above and below decks, from daylight to near darkness. When below, a pirate could switch the patch to his daylight eye and see in the darkness with the other.

---

23. Memory Like an Elephant

*B*ass remember. That's something anglers should remember when they continue throwing the same baits in the same waters with diminishing returns. In a laboratory test at Pure Fishing, Inc., Dr. Keith Jones, one of the country's foremost experts on bass behavior, allowed fish to freely strike a minnow lure for five minutes. By the end of that time the bass learned to ignore the lure "since it provided no positive food reward."

Half of those fish were then re-exposed to the same lure two weeks later. This time, interest in the lure was just one tenth of the original interest, "indicating the bass had retained a strong negative memory of the bait during the two-week interval."
After two months, the other half of the fish still tested well below the original response level.

"The results show that under some circumstances, bass can remember lures for at least up to three months and perhaps much, much longer," Jones said. "Who knows? If the experience is bad enough, they might never forget."

Concurrently, Jones discovered bass learn in four main ways:

- Associative learning or, in other words, trial and error, which is likely why bass ignored the minnow lure the second time. Also, this type of learning has been proved in lab tests "where the animal is taught to link two types of stimuli, such as certain colored light with an ensuing electric shock. Bass readily learn those associations, both in the lab and in the field, although not as fast as some other species."

- Habituation. In this type of learning, a bass gradually becomes less sensitive to particular stimulations, such as the noise of boat traffic on a busy lake.

- Spatial. Bass learn to navigate freely in home environments, recognizing landmarks or objects and staking out territories. Jones reported bass in a lab learned to find their way through a maze to a desired point.

- Prey images. Bass learn to recognize different types of forage. "Given enough positive experience with a certain prey type, a bass will gradually come to actively seek out that specific prey," he Jones said. "Prey species, for their part, often counter the bass's efforts by changing their signature stimuli, often through the use of camouflage."

---

24. Ups and Downs of Bass Parenting

*J*ust as with people, bass need stability to successfully raise their families. Stability isn't easy to achieve for even the most responsible largemouth parents. That's because the whims of nature and the needs of man often complicate or even deny the conditions necessary for a strong year class.

"Anglers need to be aware that White River fisheries are cyclical. They're going to have their ups and downs," said A.J. Pratt with the Missouri Department of Conservation. The fisheries biologist was specifically talking about Beaver, Table Rock, and Bull Shoals. But every natural lake and reservoir can prove hostile for bass in their first year.

By contrast, what conditions will yield a strong year class? I asked fisheries experts to explain, especially for reservoirs, which receive most of the angling pressure.

Not surprisingly, stable weather and water for the spawn and immediately after rank at the top. If few fry survive, then a year class is all but eliminated.

"If nests are shallow enough, then extreme cold and storms can force the males to abandon them," said Gene Gilliland, B.A.S.S. National Conservation Director. "Smallmouth and spotted bass are less likely (than largemouths) to be affected because they nest deeper."

Also, depending on the timing, wind from storms can destroy shallow-water nests or break up the fry school, making the tiny fish more vulnerable to predation, according to Mike Maceina, a fisheries professor emeritus at Auburn University. Additionally, the turbidity it creates can make finding food much more difficult.

"Mortality is very high for a week or two after the spawn anyway," Maceina said. "Mostly it's predation, but fry will die in two or three days if they don't eat. That's why each nest will have 2,000 to 3,000 eggs."

In reservoirs, falling water levels can be just as damaging as foul weather. "They can fluctuate greatly from year to year and that can make for some weak year classes," Pratt said. "But on the opposite side, if you get a lot of rain and the water stays up for an extended period, then you have good habitat (along shoreline) and an influx of nutrients," the Missouri biologist added. "That can produce a good population."

Low, stable water also can enable a good spawn. Sometimes, though, it will be more nutrient-poor than high water. Consequently, fry either won't survive or grow as quickly into robust fingerlings. Still, good year classes are possible during low water, Maceina said.

Meanwhile, water moving quickly through a reservoir can be harmful, the fisheries professor explained. "When you have a high exchange rate, then it's more like a river. You have more turbidity and food is blown out."

In natural lakes and some reservoirs, aquatic vegetation provides both food for the young fish and refuge from predation. "That's one of the most consistent factors for guaranteeing good reproduction," said Maceina, adding that too much can be nearly as harmful as too little.

Gilliland agreed. "If you have too much cover, little bass will stay in there and keep eating bugs on the plants," he said. "Then in the fall, the plants die back and the fish will be only two inches long. They're much more likely to get eaten."

Shifting to a fish diet early in the summer can enable young of the year bass to grow to six or even eight inches by fall, greatly enhancing their chances of surviving the winter.

"If you're going to grow big bass, it needs to happen quickly," Maceina said. "The growth advantage occurs early in life."

During winter, meanwhile, cover in deeper water can help young bass, especially the smaller ones, escape being eaten.

"Shallow-water cover is critical right after the spawn," Gilliland said. "But they can't stay there in winter because the water is too cold. That's why it might be a good idea to make brush rows (into deeper water) instead of brush piles."

Fisheries managers wait until the following spring to gauge the strength of a year class. "You want to see them through their first fall and winter," Gilliland said. "And size will vary hugely. As with any population, you're going to have a bell curve. Some grow like rabbits, and some are runts. The majority will be in the middle."

Sustaining fisheries

Considering everything a young bass has to endure during its first year, it's a good thing a strong class isn't necessary every year to maintain a healthy fishery. "Every several years, you need a good spawn," Gilliland said. "Bass have long lives compared to other fish. Missing a year class is not a huge hole in the population for a fish that lives ten years or more.

"But if you have two or three (poor year classes) in a row, then you have a bigger hole and anglers will notice. It will show up three or four years down the road in fewer quality fish."

Fortunately, bass are an adaptable and determined species, foul weather and fluctuating water levels notwithstanding. "Bass will spawn in a lot of different places, in a lot of different depths," the conservation director said. "And not all of them spawn at the same time. Usually there are enough successful nests to maintain the population."

25. Does Catch-and-Release Help?

*R*eleasing a bass makes us feel good. But does catch-and-release really help sustain fisheries? Based on results from a tagging study at Texas' Amon Carter, a 1,539 acre fishery north of the Dallas/ Fort Worth Metroplex, the answer is a resounding "Yes!"

Sixty-three percent of 786 tagged bass were caught. In other words, fishermen landed or boated nearly 500 of those fish. Forty-three percent were weighed in by tournament anglers. Another 16.3 percent was caught and released by recreational fishermen, with just 3.7 percent harvested.

That suggests that a bass once caught and then released— at least in some fisheries— will provide angling enjoyment a second time.

There's plenty more evidence too of the finite number of catchable bass in any given fishery and "paying it forward" by releasing at least some of the fish that you catch. Nearly 75 percent of tagged fish were caught at Florida's Lake Santa Fe.

"Another study we did on Rodman years ago was 40 percent caught by anglers," said Mike Allen, professor of Fisheries and Aquatic Sciences at the University of Florida.

On Tennessee's Norris Reservoir, meanwhile, the "adjusted annual angler catch rate" for tagged largemouth bass was 47 percent in 1996 and 34 percent in 1997.

And Jacob Westhoff encountered some powerful anecdotal evidence while doing a smallmouth telemetry study on the Jacks Fork River for the Missouri Cooperative Fish and Wildlife Unit. Eighteen of the 33 bronzebacks with transmitters were caught by anglers.

"Also of note is that eight of our fish were caught by a single angler in one day during the winter at the confluence of Alley Spring and the Jacks Fork River," he said.

Clearly, the evidence is there to support the wisdom of catch-and-release—and more.

"Those findings highlight the importance of proper fish care," said Randy Myers, a fisheries biologist for Texas Parks and Wildlife.

But he's quick to add that not all bass fisheries reveal such dramatic findings. For example, just 38 percent of more than 6,000 tagged fish were caught on Sam Rayburn, a lake more than 70 times the size of Carter. In other words, those 6,000 are a much smaller part of the population in Rayburn than they would be in Carter.

Allen added that the statewide estimate for Florida lakes is only about 20 percent. "It obviously varies widely among water bodies and probably among regions," he said. "In Florida we have so many lakes. It's probably higher in states without as many fishing sites."

Allen's point is important. The percentage of a bass population caught ties directly to angling pressure. At Amon Carter, tournament and recreational effort was a combined 14 hours per acre, while that figure was 5.2 at Rayburn. And in Florida drought had reduced accessible areas at other fisheries, likely forcing more anglers than normal to fish Santa Fe.

Other factors can also influence how great a percentage is caught. "Rayburn has better habitat than Carter," Myers said. "Overall, it's a better lake for bass production."

Still, angling pressure is a top consideration for resource managers in maintaining healthy bass fisheries. That's why Myers is hopeful that removal of a protective slot at Ray Roberts will attract tournaments away from Carter.

"At Carter, more than half of the effort was from tournament anglers," he said. "Because they're so popular, we have to think long and hard about restrictions that would limit tournaments. But if 50 percent of tournament-retained fish die (at Carter) it would have some impact on the fishery."

Consequently, how fish are cared for before being released is also a concern for Myers and other fisheries managers. "If a fish is gilling, lots of experienced anglers still assume it will live," Myers said. "But that's not always true. Some of those fish do die."

The Texas biologist pointed to statistics gathered as part of a fizzing study during five tournaments at Lake Amistad in 2009. On days when the water temperature was in the 50s and 60s, mortality, both immediate and delayed, was less than 10 percent. On a day when the temperature was 79 to 80, total mortality was 23 percent and delayed 18.3. And, most sobering, when the temperature was 83, total mortality was 50.8 percent and delayed 42.1.

"What we saw at Amistad is that 75 degrees is the critical temperature for bass health in a livewell," he said. "That high mortality was strictly related to water temperature."

Hot days and heavy limits

Research like that at Amistad prompted Texas biologists Randy Myers and James Driscoll to recommend an oxygen injection system for livewells, particularly when an angler has a hefty limit, as often happens at Texas reservoirs.

"Oxygen injection has long been used by Texas Parks and Wildlife Department hatcheries to maintain the health of fish being stocked into reservoirs," they said.

"Fisheries' staff regularly transport or hold fish in ratios equal to or greater than one pound of fish to a gallon of water. However, boat manufactures do not offer oxygen injection system options and very few tournament anglers have installed oxygen equipment on their boats."

Proper installation and operation of such a system, they added, "will ensure oxygen levels remain above the preferred level of 7 milligrams per liter, even when livewells contain heavy limits."

26. Hear, Hear!
Fish Talk About Sex

Who knew?

Fish talk. And often they talk about sex.

Of course, they don't "speak" in words because they don't have vocal cords. Rather, they are "soniferous," meaning they make sounds. They use their teeth, bladders, and other means to grunt, croak, click, drum, and squeak, saying things like "Swim over here, fishy, fishy" and "Get outta here, you fat flounder. This is my nest."

Up to 1,000 species of fish are believed to be chatty and, yes, the sunfish family, which includes bass, is part of the conversation.

In fact, hydrophones were used to study bluegill courtships sounds more than 40 years ago. "Some centrarchids do make noise," said Gene Wilde, professor of fish ecology at Texas Tech. "But it seems to be only during breeding season and we're not sure how they do it. Possibly by rubbing mouth parts together.

"Some species make sounds year around," he added. "But most fish sounds are associated with breeding. For example, drum attract mates that way."

The gizzard shad, an important forage fish, is one species that makes sounds year around, and something a Texas Tech graduate student recently discovered about those sounds when the fish are exposed to environmental stressors is significant.

"Gizzard shad are widespread, in about two thirds of the country," said Matt Gruntorad. "They produce calls when stressed, and these calls could be an early warning system when there's a (water quality) problem. They could help protect valuable game fish and water supplies."

The Texas Tech researcher exposed the shad to various levels of salinity, pH, and toxicity (ammonia hydroxide). As levels increased, the fish became louder—up to a point. At the highest levels they became quieter. "There could be a threshold when they're too stressed to make sounds," Gruntorad said.

Sounds made by fish of two inches or so were too soft to analyze. But 12-inch shad yielded strong signals for the hydrophones. Even so, their calls would be difficult, if not impossible, for the human ear to detect.

"They don't croak," the graduate student said. "Their calls are simple and very quiet. They release gas through the anal duct. It's like a fish fart."

Compared to saltwater, much work remains to be done to recognize and understand sounds made by fish in freshwater, Gruntorad said.

Wilde agreed, adding that drum make their unique sound by playing muscles against their swim bladders, while catfish create their characteristic "grunts" by rubbing the pectoral spine against the pectoral girdle. "Smaller fish click their teeth together," he said.

The fish behavior expert also said any fish sound an angler hears above the water isn't the same as what would be heard underwater.

"It's tough for people to hear fish noises (in the water)," he explained. "For schooling fish, like herring, sound is a close-range thing to keep the integrity of the school."

With tongue planted firmly in cheek, Wilde assured animal rights activists that fish do not scream when hooked. "We put a hydrophone in a phone where we catch a lot of bass," he said. "And that did not happen."

Eavesdropping

One reason the learning curve regarding soniferous fish improved in recent years is that researchers modified their diving gear. For years they were unaware of conversations because sounds of bubbles released by SCUBA gear masked them, as well as frightened the fish.

Now researchers use self-contained breathing systems with no gas bubbles released. "Increasingly scientists are discovering unusual mechanisms by which fish make and hear secret whispers, grunts, and thumps to attract mates and ward off the enemy," said *LiveScience*.com.

"In just one bizarre instance, seahorses create clicks by tossing their heads. They snap the rear edge of their skulls against their star-shaped bony crests."

Meanwhile, the swim bladder, also used to control buoyancy, is one of the most common instruments for fish sounds. A muscle attached to the swim bladder contracts and relaxes in rapid sequence, causing the organ to produce a low-pitched drumming sound.

Some species use stridulation, pushing teeth and/or bones together. And still others use body movements to make sounds by altering water flow.

Fish hearing

Yes, fish have ears—of a sort. Actually they possess ear bones known as *otoliths*. Also used to age fish, these bones vary in shape and size according to species, just as human ears vary from one person to another. However, fish otoliths can't be seen externally.

Sound travels through water as waves or vibrations and because a fish's body is of similar density, the sound waves pass through it. But they cause the ear bones to vibrate.

Additionally, a fish can sense vibrations and movement with its *lateral line*, a sensory organ consisting of fluid-filled sacs with hairlike cells, open through a series of pores along the side.

But because sound travels farther and 4.4 times faster in water than in air, a fish can struggle to hear through the "clutter" of outboard engines and recreational activity, according to Hydrowave, which makes a sound device designed to attract bass and other game fish by imitating the sound of baitfish and predatory fish feeding on them.

"This speed, combined with the poor visibility characteristics of water is the reason a fish is so dependent on vibration and water displacement . . . for location of prey," the company said.

"The source of sound clutter is always present. This forms the basis of how fish have developed keen senses that allow them to specifically identify clutter from prey and feeding activities of other fish."

Four-time Classic winner Kevin VanDam said the Hydrowave works in two ways. "It excites fish because they hear the sound of other bass eating," he explained. "And it excites the bait. It draws it up."

Hydrowave sound tracks include Feeding Frenzy, Schooling, Passive Finesse, Fleeing Bait, Bait Frenzy, and Bait Panic.

27. Angler's Advantage: Bass as Chameleons

*B*ass might have big mouths, but they don't exaggerate.

In fact, black bass are masters of understatement, at least regarding their appearance. Boasting brilliant hues and/or electric highlights, some fish are among nature's most spectacular creatures. But in a world of green water with green vegetation, largemouth bass evolved as green fish. Likewise, their brown cousins, the smallmouth bass, molded themselves to a watery world of gravel and rock.

This camouflage helps protect bass from larger predators and enables them to more easily ambush prey. And Mother Nature didn't stop there. Like aquatic chameleons, bass can alter that shading, which helped solidify their reputation as North America's most versatile game fish.

"Bass adapt to their surroundings. If they didn't, they would starve," said Ben Beck, director of the U.S. Department of Agriculture's Aquatic Animal Health Research Unit at Auburn University.

"Bass don't think about it. They just do it," added Gene Gilliland, National Conservation Director for B.A.S.S.

But color change doesn't occur spontaneously in bass as it does in other species. "The chameleon and the octopus can rapidly change," Beck said. "Bass can adapt. We're just not sure how fast the process works."

Florida's Wes Porak, a black bass genetics expert, added, "These responses are fairly rapid and affect the color patterns when the changes occur. A fish can change color within half an hour if placed in a lighted or dark tank after being collected from a lake."

Savvy anglers are quick to turn this adaptive ability to their own advantage (see below), but fisheries scientists still have much to discover about the biological mechanism for change in bass, as most research is focused on colorful reef and tropical fishes. That's understandable too, when considering how monotonous the black bass is in appearance, even compared to its cousin the bluegill—especially during the spawning season.

"Not a lot is known about bass and it's tricky to get a scientist to say anything definitive," Beck explained. "They're still under study."

Porak admitted he has "a limited understanding about how the intensity of a fish's pigment can change based on the amount of light striking parts of the retina and also the skin of a fish."

Before exploring what little is known and/or suspected, let's look at the basic coloration of a largemouth bass. The Florida Museum of Natural History (FMNH) describes it this way: "The back and head are dark green to light green in color with lighter sides and a whitish belly and underside of the head."

It adds that a prominent lateral stripe runs from the snout through the eye to the base of the tail. "Towards the tail, there is a series of blotches of varying sizes. These blotches evolve into a solid, even stripe on the caudal peduncle (narrow part of the body).

. . Vertical fins lightly pigmented, paired fins generally clear; caudal fin alike in young and adult."

Whether they're in Lake Okeechobee, the Mississippi River, or the California Delta, largemouth bass share that basic color pattern. But as any angler who has fished all three will tell you, they don't look the same.

"Genetic components influence appearance some and food does a little," Gilliland said. "But water color, clarity, and habitat have a bigger influence. That's why fish will blush out in muddy water and look more camouflaged in vegetation."

Hormones seem to be the key to these variations, according to Beck. "Photo receptors (in the eye) set the biological clock," he said. "They tell light from dark, and they tell the hormones to change colors."

He added that "generic stressors," such as confinement in a livewell, may also cause change, typically making the fish look more washed out, just as it would from living in turbid water. Either way, hormones likely trigger the alteration, with bass turning lighter when pigment granules aggregate deeper in the skin and darker when they disperse nearer the surface.

In general, the deeper a bass and/or the muddier the water it lives in, the lighter its color will be, due to less penetration by sunlight—even to the point that the lateral line seems to disappear. The shallower and/or more clear the water, the darker the fish will be. Additionally, more alkaline water—usually indicative of fisheries with no vegetation—can make a bass less vivid. By contrast, bass in vegetation-filled waters (more acidic) often boast sharper camouflaging.

In tannic (brown) water, fish can still be dark if it doesn't block light penetration, Gilliland said. But in black water, often caused by decaying vegetation, bass will be more washed out.

And this from the FMNH: "Adults from mud-bottom lakes are dark olive brown to black, with markings hardly distinguishable. Males in breeding condition tend to be darker in overall color."

Plus, researchers noted that Lake Erie smallmouth bass transform from a mottled color when they're resting at night to a more uniform pattern when they're moving. That's because the contrasting pattern works as camouflage when a bass is near the bottom, but makes it more visible (and consequently less efficient as a predator) when it's moving, they hypothesized.

Gilliland concluded, "Color changes in bass are evolutionary advantages. If a smallmouth is feeding in shallow water he will color himself to blend into the bottom so shiners don't see him when they look down. It's all part of the predatory process."

Angler's advantage

If you understand how water depth, clarity, and vegetation can alter a fish's appearance, you'll have a good idea of where to fish next when the bite stops.

For example, you catch a bass on a topwater in open water. If its sides are dark, it's likely a shallow schooler and you'll have to move to find the fish again. But if the sides are pale it probably came from deepwater to grab your bait, and there are likely more bass where that one came from. Only most, especially the big ones, aren't willing to expend the energy to chase food on top. Try working the depths with a crankbait or soft plastic.

Or what if you're catching fish along a dropoff near a weedline? If the color is especially rich and sharp, the bass probably came out of the grass to eat your bait. That could suggest you'll catch more fish nearer or in the grass, where that camouflage makes them effective ambush predators. If the color pattern isn't as clearly defined, a deeper presentation closer to the dropoff might be better.

It's also important to remember that forage species also use camouflage to help them avoid bass and other sport fish. Often they use "countershading," which means a dark back, to better blend into the bottom, and a white belly to better match the lighter background above—especially if a predator is looking up. Generally, anglers believe they should "match the hatch" with baits that have dark backs and light bellies to make their offerings more natural looking. But a counter argument holds that if you use a bait with coloration just the opposite, bass will more readily see and strike it. The jury is still out.

Odd balls

Have you heard about those "gold" bass caught from time to time? This condition, known as *xanthism*, is the most striking aberration in bass appearance. It also occurs in other fish, as well as reptiles and birds.

Considered a genetic mutation, a bass with xanthism lacks the ability to convert white light to blue in its molecular structures. That blue normally combines with yellow to make green.

"It's rare, but not unheard of," said Gene Gilliland, National Conservation Director for B.A.S.S. "I've seen it in other sunfish. But talk about a target. A fish that color has little chance of survival. If it does survive, it beats some crazy odds."

Meanwhile, bass with black blotches aren't quite so rare, especially in clear, northern waters. "What literally happens is, accumulations of melanin-producing cells aggregate in the dermis and epidermis of the fish," said Geoffrey Smith, Susquehanna River biologist for the Pennsylvania Boat and Fish Commission. "The bigger question is why this happens, and is it really happening more frequently, or just being observed more frequently?"

Smith is especially interested in learning more about this condition because anglers often report catching smallmouth bass with black blotches from the Susquehanna, a river troubled by water quality problems and a declining fishery.

Some scientists suspect endocrine disruption may be a cause of the blotches, and that could be caused, at least in some cases, by pollutants.

Disappearing act

As with bass, other fish, especially forage species, have evolved with appearance adaptations to help them survive. "Some juvenile fish have colors that help them hide from prey," said Auburn's Ben Beck. "Some fish have false eye spots to trick predators. And some baitfish are iridescent, which allows them to communicate with each other and move in unison."

This makes it much more difficult for bass and other predators to target individual fish.

As previously described, countershading also helps. When seen from the top the darker dorsal area of the fish blends into the bottom or darkness of the water below. When viewed from below, the lighter ventral area blends into the light filtering down from the surface.

Appearance also helps protect some species because of what the predator has learned to associate with a particular color. For example, bass show a decided preference for the tadpoles of spring peepers, which are brown, over the tadpoles of toads, which are black.

---

28. What's On the Menu for Bass?

*G*iven the chance, these versatile and adaptable predators will eat insects, invertebrates, and most any fish species small enough to swallow, from rainbow trout in California to hornpout in New England. Birds, mice, frogs, snakes, lizards, and ducklings have all met an untimely demise in the bellies of opportunistic largemouth bass.

However, bluegill and shad provide most of the fuel that powers America's No. 1 sport fish. But which of the two most benefits bass, and consequently, bass anglers?

Neither. And both.

"For bluegill, the primary benefit is their abundance," said Dan Shoup, associate professor of fisheries ecology at Oklahoma State University. "Bass are often opportunistic foragers and when bluegill are numerically abundant, that means they end up being eaten regularly."

He added, "Shad also have high abundance in some systems, so, just like with bluegill, a largemouth bass will often eat a lot of shad simply because they're easy to find."

This bass was dining on threadfin shad

Still, the advantage goes to bluegill because their needs and preferences closely mirror those of its larger sunfish cousin. In fact, waters with bass and no bluegill are the exception rather than the rule, from the smallest farm pond to Lake Superior.

"Bluegill often hang out in the same habitats as bass since both are cover-oriented species," Shoup said. "Even a moderate density of bluegill ends up being an easy choice for bass because they occur in large aggregations in places the bass are frequently located, such as brushpiles."

On the other hand, shad inhabit open water and are most numerous in large lakes and impoundments. While bass will eat them year around, during summer and winter they're most likely to move from shoreline cover to deep-water structure and target shad. Sometimes they follow these schooling fish. Bluegill might have the overall abundance advantage, but hungry bass can more quickly eat their fill by slashing into these concentrations of shad.

As they do so, bass get more bang for their buck. Advantage to shad.

"Think high-calorie food, which to a wild animal is a good thing as they tend not to be concerned about their waistlines," said Shoup. "Shad have a higher lipid content than most species, which makes them a more energetically valuable food."

Also, shad are easier to swallow. Literally.

"Bluegill have a rather effective anti-predator behavior where they simply stick up their spines and orient at a 90-degree angle to the bass," the Oklahoma State fisheries expert said. "The spines make them quite a bit harder to handle than other species like shad, cisco, or minnow species."

Also, bluegill have large girths compared to length, and those spines are positioned along the deepest part of the body. "Bluegill almost have to be oriented head-first (for the bass) to swallow, and the length of bluegill that can be handled is pretty short compared to other species that don't have as deep a body," Shoup said. "So bluegill can outgrow bass a little faster and easier than other species with a similar growth rate, simply because they have a deep body.

"This makes bluegill useful as a food source for only a few years, as opposed to (yellow) perch, which might be edible even when they are quite long."

Size may also be a negative for one species of shad. "Gizzard shad can be great in a trophy bass situation, but they really aren't forage because they grow faster than bass," said Gene Gilliland, B.A.S.S. National Conservation Director. "Threadfin shad are better because they spawn later and don't get as big."

Shoup echoed that assessment, pointing out that gizzard shad can easily reach more than 12 inches in length. "As such, gizzard shad often outgrow the gape limitation (mouth size) bass can handle by the time they're just one year old. Yet they may live 6 to 10 years, so most of their life span is spent being too large to eat.

"Threadfin grow more slowly and are typically vulnerable for most of their lives," he added. "This makes threadfin a better forage base in systems where they can overwinter without high mortality."

Gilliland said that area typically is not much farther north than Interstate 40, which runs from North Carolina through Arkansas and on to southern California. Bull Shoals and Table Rock on the Missouri-Arkansas border are a couple of notable exceptions, as are power plant impoundments. Unlike the much hardier gizzard shad, threadfin will start to die in water of about 40 degrees.

While bluegill and threadfin shad provide most of the fuel to produce quality bass fisheries, too much of either can be a bad thing.

"Both prey species compete with juvenile bass for food," Shoup explained. "As such, fishery managers must perform a balancing act. You want ample for forage, but not if it causes your predator species to grow slowly as juveniles."

For example, in many fisheries juvenile bluegill compete with juvenile bass for zooplankton and insect larvae throughout most of the first growing season. If food is abundant enough, by late summer bass can reach three to four inches, large enough to start eating other fish. But if cover is too dense . . .

"Lots of research shows adult bass are poor at capturing bluegill once the density of cover gets above some threshold level," the fisheries scientist said. "This can create a stunted bluegill fishery because bluegill do not grow well when they're hiding from bass like this. This doesn't help the bass population, even though the bluegill stay small enough to eat for a greater number of years, because the bass have a hard time capturing the bluegill."

Additionally, bluegill are notorious egg predators, which hampers reproduction in systems where bluegill abundance is too high.

Shad, meanwhile, also compete for zooplankton. "You can actually lose a whole year class of bass if shad densities are too high," Shoup said. "Shad can produce a zooplankton crash just before juvenile bass need to start eating zooplankton."

Additionally, over-abundant shad can increase turbidity. "Because bass are primarily visual feeders, their foraging return drops quite a big as turbidity increases," he added. "This can lead to slow growth and/or poor condition in some systems where shad are abundant."

Best size bait for bass?

"When you look at bass diets in the field, you rarely see any size of bass frequently eat prey near the maximum size they could eat," said Dan Shoup, an Oklahoma State fisheries expert. "Most eat prey that are considerably smaller."

That's probably because larger prey move faster and require more energy to capture than smaller forage. Related to that, a higher escape rate makes it more likely the bass will expend energy with no pay-off at the end.

"Larger bass will definitely eat larger prey," he emphasized. "But it isn't uncommon to find a 5-pound bass eating 3- or 4-inch bluegill even though they could handle much larger prey if they wanted.

"Ultimately, there's a tradeoff for a predator picking prey sizes. Going after large prey requires more energy/effort and has a lower success rate, but a big pay-off when successful. But going too small means you must eat a lot more to get full, even if capturing them is relatively easy. Each item you strike at takes time and energy, so things tend to optimize with mid-size prey as the best bang for the buck."

Other options

While bluegill and shad provide the most important prey for bass overall, plenty of other fish species are notable as well, including non-native blueback herring, alewife, and round goby. The first two are difficult to distinguish from one another and often collectively known as "river herring."

A species that spawns in freshwater, the blueback herring has expanded its range in New York through ship locks and canals. Other states have intentionally introduced the species, including Virginia, Georgia, Tennessee, and the Carolinas. Preferring deep, open water, it can grow to 12 inches, with a silvery body that is deep bluish-green on the back. In some fisheries a decrease in game fish coincided with introduction of this species, and fisheries managers suspect the herring not only preys on the eggs and larvae of native fish, but also competes with them for zooplankton. On the other hand, many anglers believe the herring provide a nutritional boost for some bass fisheries.

The alewife's biology and history are similar, although it's mostly established in the Great Lakes, with a few scattered introductions to the south. The alewife was first noted in Lake Ontario more than a century ago and likely gained entry to the other lakes through the Welland Canal during the 1930s. Reaching six to seven inches at maturity, it is more noted as forage for salmon and trout than bass. Alewives also compete with native species for zooplankton and eat eggs and larvae.

Introduced in the ballast water of ocean-going ships, the round goby is mostly a Great Lakes occupant, although it has been found in nearby inland waters. First discovered in the St. Clair River in 1990, the round goby has spread rapidly since then. Growing to about ten inches, they are prolific and spawn several times a year. They compete with native species for habitat and also feed on their eggs and young. They are notorious bait stealers. On the plus side, anecdotal evidence suggests smallmouth bass are growing faster and larger because of goby diets.

29. What I Learned in Florida

*A*h, Florida, the Sunshine State. The name tells you everything. It never gets cold in Florida, right?

Wrong!

The coldest I've ever been on the water was on central Florida's Butler Chain on a bright, sunny day in January. We were on the backside of low pressure, pushed out by a blast of frigid air from the northwest. My nose felt like a popsicle. My frigid fingers became useless appendages. My parka seemed to provide no warmth at all—although I knew it did. And the day was interminable, as the bass refused to bite even shiners.

Of course, "cold" is relative. I've been fishing in Midwest states when air temperatures were far lower than the 35 to 40 degrees they were that day, but I was much more comfortable. Something about cold in Florida, especially on the water, makes it exceptionally wicked.

Perhaps it's psychological. It's not supposed to be chilly down there. Your mind rejects reality, and your body pays the price.

Trust me on this. If decide to go fishing in Florida from December through March, take plenty of warm clothing, just in case. And, yes, I mean even as far south as Lake Okeechobee. I've seen frost down there early in the morning. The saving grace is that cold spells are typically short-lived. And even on days that start out frigid, the air can warm quickly once the sun is high.

Here's what else I've learned in Florida:

1. Florida-strain largemouth bass don't like the cold either, but they still bite.

Common knowledge has it that the Florida strain is more difficult to catch than the northern strain. Possibly that's true. But my theory is that those Sunshine State fish, living mostly in shallow water, are simply less cold tolerant. A temperature drop of just a few degrees from one day to the next can temporarily shut them down. And if a cold front moves in, as happened that day on the Butler Chain, they really get a case of lockjaw.

Or do they?

Captain Pete Matson and I were fishing Kenansville Lake, west of Vero Beach, on such a day. Averaging about three feet in depth, the impoundment is filled with vegetation, and just about requires you throw Texas-rigged soft plastics. And that's what we did, often changing baits in hopes of finding one the bass would bite. We failed.

Also, we moved often, finally pushing into pads with sparse grass growing underneath. Neither one of us was a fan of flipping, but finally Pete decided to try it, even though there was no edge and the water beneath us was just as shallow as most other places. In other words, flipping meant dropping the bait nearly straight down from the boat.

Pete dropped a critter bait and—bam! He boated our first fish of the day. Still, we refused to believe it could be that simple.

But another drop produced another fish and I joined in the action. We now knew bass were in water all around us so we tried casting again and slowing our retrieves to a virtual crawl. Nothing.

Either the fish bit on a vertical drop, right beside the boat, or they didn't bite at all.

That trip on a cold winter's day in Florida convinced me that flipping can not only be a productive technique, but sometimes it's the only way to get fish to bite.

2. Sometimes you almost can't retrieve fast enough.

By contrast, on a warm, but rainy day, we expected fish to be active on Lake Jackson in Highlands County. They were, but we couldn't catch them. They weren't interested in topwaters or plastics dragged on the bottom. They'd follow spinnerbaits. We could see their wakes in the shallows. But they wouldn't take.

Sometimes, slowing down the retrieve will entice a hesitant bass to bite. But these fish were active, chasing bait as well as shadowing our spinnerbaits. I decided to speed up the retrieve, and two casts later caught our first fish.

Encouraged, I tried even faster, and the bass liked it even better. Eventually we caught fish consistently by burning those spinnerbaits over the top of the water just as fast as we could reel them in. And I suspect that those actively feeding fish would have continued pouncing on our offerings if we could have retrieved them even faster.

I've since learned that, at best, most of us are reeling at 2 to 5 miles an hour, even when we're hastily bringing in a bait to make another cast. On the other hand, bass can swim at bursts of 12 to 18 miles an hour. Burning a bait for us equals just a jog for them.

3. Sometimes there are more important things than catching fish.

At least for some people. Not me.

During a float trip in Alaska I followed the advice of my guides and bought a head net to protect myself from black flies and gnats that can be brutal up that way during summer. The net worked well and I started carrying it with me no matter where I went fishing.

My Florida friends teased me about it because I stored it the crown of a wide-brimmed hat and, admittedly, the combination did look funny.

Then came that fateful day when we were catching one bass after another on Rat-L-Traps on the Kissimmee Chain in an open stretch of water surrounded by hydrilla. The day was warm and sunny, but a slight breeze kept us comfortable.

Then the wind died, and the hydrilla gnats moved in. I had never encountered them before, but quickly realized the head net would be a good idea. We kept fishing and I wasn't bothered in the least by the bug invasion. But my friends, who only minutes before were kidding me for the upteenth time about my funny hat, started waving, slapping, coughing, and hacking at the gnats. Eventually, they could no longer tolerate the infestation and we had to leave. Since the boat belonged to one of them, I had no say in the matter.

Over the years I've been extremely conscientious about reminding them of that incident and how we had to leave a great bite because they weren't man enough to ignore a few swarming insects.

4. Even if the day is sunny, don't trust the weather.

During a pleasant, partly cloudy day in summer, a friend from New Jersey and I were fishing the Clermont Chain with a friend who lives there. In fact, we were just a few hundred yards from his boat house. This was my New Jersey friend's first trip to Florida, while I considered the Sunshine State my second home.

Suddenly our New Jersey friend asked, "What does it mean when your line is standing straight up?"

Stunned by the question, my Florida friend and I quickly turned to see that, indeed, his 10-pound test was hanging in the air above his graphite rod.

"It means we get off the water right now!" the two of us yelled simultaneously.

We scooted into the boat house just as a tremendous boom shattered the peaceful day. Even with the sun shining and no rain falling, lightning had just struck someplace close to us.

Florida well deserves its reputation as "lightning capital of the United States." (The African country of Rwanda owns the world title.) And central Florida, from Tampa to Titusville, is "lightning alley." Lightning storms occur an average of 100 days per year in this area, which was right where we were fishing.

5. If you're topwater fishing at night, don't automatically assume what's pulling on the other end of your line is a bass.

And in a related corollary, remember that virtually every body of freshwater in Florida is home to an alligator or two. Coincidentally, they are nocturnal feeders.

PART FOUR: Management and Stewardship

The author in Florida

---

30. Shocking Discoveries from Electrofishing

*E*lectrofishing is the primary tool used by fisheries biologists in most states to assess bass populations. "It is fast, efficient, and non-lethal," said Gene Gilliland, National Conservation Director for B.A.S.S., former fisheries biologist, and avid angler.

"It allows us to catch large numbers of fish for length, weight, growth, and diet information," added Georgia's Jim Hakala. "It allows us to see how well the fish are growing, weak and strong year classes, average fish size, how robust the population is, and often, at what size anglers begin to pick up the harvest on a certain bass species."

Resource managers, aren't the only ones who can benefit from this tool. "If I have a choice of going electrofishing or fishing, I learn more from electrofishing," said Georgia guide Mike Bucca, who recalled assisting Hakala on Lake Allatoona.

"I couldn't find a pattern for the life of me on the south end," he recalled. "Jim was going to electrofish on the north end. We found this one pocket in which I'll bet we got over 200 fish in a one-acre spot. They were busting shad even after we went through the area.

"I made a living off that pocket for about three months, before the fish finally moved off."

Not surprisingly, joining biologists on the water is the best way for anglers to profit from electrofishing, especially for locating concentrations of fish. But any angler can improve his chances simply by picking the brains of Gilliland, Hakala, and other biologists who electrofish.

Some discoveries are of seasonal value:

Hakala once found frogs in the bellies of largemouth bass in February. "I figured the frogs they were eating were starting to emerge from the mud on the lake bottom," he theorized. "As the frogs stirred they became easy prey for largemouths. So the potential for an angler to throw a sinking frog imitation and be successful in February, when frog patterns aren't on an angler's mind, was potentially identified by the diet study."

Other valuable information is timeless:

"There are many times more bass out there than you could ever imagine," said Gilliland He explained that an electrofishing boat can make a pass down a shoreline and then a make second pass, collecting fish missed the first time.

"I guarantee that if I can't shock them all in one pass, you can't catch them all in one pass either," he said. "If you catch a bass, fish that area again. That fish was there for a reason.

"Something attracted it to that area and chances are there are more bass in the same vicinity, attracted for the same reasons."

That strategy, he added, should also apply to a single piece of cover. Many likely looking stumps, bushes, and laydowns yield no fish to the shocker, but one, for no apparent reason, might give up four or five bass.

"If you catch a bass, fish that cover thoroughly and make it a point to visit that spot again later in the day."

Fish in thick cover, he added, often have food in their stomachs. He believes that's because they've been out foraging and returned to a safe place to digest their meals. Bass in open areas, however, often have empty bellies "because they're actively searching for that next meal."

To profit from this electrifying insight, throw a fast-moving bait between clumps of weeds and brush, especially during peak feeding periods of dawn and dusk, Gilliland advised.

"On the other hand, trying to entice a bass that has a full belly out of his hiding spot may take a great deal more patience," the conservation director said. "Choose your lures and presentation accordingly."

And just what are the contents of those full bellies? Bucca was startled to see the forked tails of large gizzard shad sticking out of the throats of 4- and 5-pound spotted bass.

But Hakala said he is more often surprised by how small the forage is. "I think a lot of times they (bass) select for a certain size prey that's much smaller than what they can handle," he said. "But if something large isn't acting right, they make take the opportunity to hammer it. If the large prey was acting normally, the trigger to strike may not be there.

"That's probably why swimbaits perform well on big fish. A big fish has the means to routinely eat something large, but doesn't until that large prey is in distress. Then it pounces."

ROBERT MONTGOMERY

31. Barotrauma and the Livewell: Taking Care of Fizzness

*A*uthor's note: As Conservation Director for the New York B.A.S.S. Nation, Barb Elliott has been explaining to anglers for years what barotrauma is and how to treat it. Specializing in both live presentations and videos, the "barotrauma babe" recently made a video in French and is contemplating doing another in Japanese. Whether you're a tournament or recreational angler, you should be a good steward for our fisheries and know how to "fizz," or deflate the swim bladder, when necessary.

Take it away, Barb:

* * * * *

Barotrauma is defined as a change in air pressure, typically affecting the ear or the lung. In fishing, barotrauma is over-inflation of the swim bladder caused by bringing a fish up to atmospheric pressure at the surface of the water. It can happen to any species of fish—salt or freshwater—that possess a swim bladder.

Picture a balloon filled with air. If you took an inflated balloon deeper down the water column, it would noticeably shrink. As you brought the balloon back up to the surface it would expand to its original dimensions. The water column is actual weight that presses on the fish– compressing everything, but especially gases that are in the swim bladder.

Freshwater fish usually don't need any type of treatment if you immediately release them. They have enough energy and strength to overcome their buoyancy and swim back to their proper depth, where their bladders will deflate.

Problems with barotrauma begin when we hold fish in livewells for hours and hours. That contributes to other stressors, such as being confined and being held out of the water for measuring and possibly photos. However, before you poke a hole in the side of a bass to deflate the bladder, you should make certain that livewell conditions are optimal in terms of dissolved oxygen, temperature, and water quality.

Myth: The speed you bring the fish to the surface does not make a difference to the degree the swim bladder expands. On the contrary, the longer the fish is angled, the more energy is expended and the closer the fish is to exhaustion, meaning the bladder will expand more.

Myth: A fish cannot have barotrauma if it is caught shallow. You don't know whether that bass you just caught in five feet of water recently came out of 35 feet to feed. Any fish can suffer from barotrauma and need relief/fizzing if you plan on holding it in a livewell.

This brings up the importance of checking and rechecking throughout the day. It's especially critical to check on the health of fish for the first 15 minutes or so after you put them in the livewell.

What are the signs of barotrauma? Bass give you clear signs they're suffering, and you need to act quickly to ensure their welfare.

A fish that is on its side or upside down at the water's surface each time you open the livewell needs treatment. And it needs relief now, not at the weigh-in hours later. Damage to internal organs can start the minute you lift the fish from the water.

Fizzing, or relieving barotrauma, is an easily mastered technique. To deflate the swim bladder, use a small gauge hypodermic needle, equipped with a reamer (to keep tissue from plugging the needle), to pierce the skin of the fish at predetermined points on the side, depending on the species of fish. This releases excess gases and returns the fish to neutral buoyancy. *Bassmaster.com* and other websites can show you where to place the needle and provide more detailed instruction.

Neutral buoyancy is the point at which the fish neither sinks nor floats. This is the most important part of the technique to learn, and can only be determined while the fish is in the water. You do not release gas for a certain amount of time, nor do you count to three or five or whatever. You withdraw the needle at the point the fish no longer sinks or floats.

As with all techniques, fizzing has evolved. Initially it was accomplished by targeting the swim bladder through the open mouth of the fish. Although this accomplished the goal by relieving excess gas, it also put the bass at risk. That's because major organs are clustered around the gullet and at risk of being pierced as well. One of those is the rete miribal, which regulates gas into and out of the bladder. If it's damaged, the fish won't ever be able to regulate its buoyancy again.

People often have a difficult time adjusting to new things/techniques. Using side penetration in barotrauma relief has been no different. I've been educating people in this technique developed by Canadian researcher Steven Cooke for more than six years, and I am constantly amazed at the number of people who have yet to adjust to this improved method.

As responsible anglers we must take good care of our tournament-held fish so they're viable when we release them. Viable fish go on after the tournament to eat, grow, and reproduce. They live on to replenish the population. All responsible tournament anglers should strive for this goal.

Do your homework and keep up with latest fish care research. If you aren't sure where to find such information, contact your state B.A.S.S. Nation conservation director. He or she can help.

32. Taking Care of Bassness: Catch and Release Basics

*A*uthor's note: A passionate advocate for proper fish care, Judy Tipton is founder of New Pro Products and inventor of the V-T2 Livewell Ventilation System, an accessory that provides a more natural and healthier environment for fish held in a livewell. I asked her to provide examples of how anglers can better care for the bass they catch, to ensure that they live to fight another day. Here's what she said:

*　　*　　*　　*　　*

As anglers we all have little tricks to catch more fish. But when it comes to fish care, we need to do away with tricks and look to solid science and the biological needs of fish. None of us would go to a doctor who didn't have the proper education and training in health care. So, as anglers, let's not try to guess what's good for fish and their health. Knowing how to catch fish doesn't equal understanding how best care for their health.

The author saying farewell to a bass

Nosing into the bank

At mostly local and regional tournaments where anglers are responsible for returning their fish to the lake immediately after being weighed at the scales, it isn't uncommon to see the released fish nosed back into the bank in shallow water. And you'll see anglers doing their best to swirl the fish around and then push them off into deeper water, believing they're helping the fish. Although this is well-meaning , it's actually best to leave the fish alone.

Fish nose back into the bank because they're oxygen deprived. They move back to shallow for two reasons: A good level of oxygen exists at the surface of the lake because of atmospheric diffusion. And bass use the bottom of the lake to support themselves in an upright position as they recover.

Tricks to stop bleeding

A bass bleeding profusely from the gills makes any angler nervous about the risk of a penalty for a dead fish. Tricks to staunch the flow include pouring a soft drink or livewell additive on the wound. No studies have been done to understand how much damage is done to the gill structure by this practice.

A fish's gills are semi-permeable single-cell membranes used for respiration and excretion of gases. These are very delicate structures and altering or damaging them can reduce a fish's ability to extract needed oxygen or expel harmful gases from its body and lead to delayed-mortality.

No doubt anglers want to address the issue of bleeding. But until a better method of delivery and a safe and proven substance is available, it's best to simply return the fish to the water as quickly as possible. This will slow bleeding as well.

Filling livewell completely full

Some anglers plug the overflow drains on their livewells to let water in the well fill to over-capacity. The water is actually allowed to flow over the top and out from under the lids. The reasoning behind this is anglers realize fish take a beating in the livewell during rough water conditions. They hope more water in their livewells will minimize sloshing of the water and protect the fish from being thrown about.

Unfortunately, this tactic probably isn't as effective as anglers believe because of inertia. Bass in the livewell aren't attached to the water in the livewell. When movement of the boat or water changes, the fish will continue moving in the previous state of motion.

What happens when you're riding in a car and the brakes are suddenly applied? Your body wants to continue forward. That's why we wear seat belts.

Also, keeping your livewell full to over-capacity decreases the space between the water and lid. Having adequate space is very important for gas exchange. Air flow through this space enables oxygen diffusion and helps strip harmful gases such as CO_2 and ammonia from the water. It also will keep the livewell from experiencing a super-saturation of dissolved oxygen and prevent gas bubble disease in the fish from pressurized oxygen systems.

Finally, water has high specific heat. Air space allows heat to rise off the water, helping maintaining cooler temperatures in the livewell.

* * * * *

Following is an explanation of the V-T2. It is a livewell accessory so simple in design that many anglers have difficulty believing it can enhance bass survival. It can and does, which is why it has been endorsed by B.A.S.S. Conservation.

* * * * *

The easily installed V-T2, with no moving parts, creates an open air exchange when placed in the center of a livewell lid. A three-inch sleeve protrudes into the water, directing air into, through, and out of the livewell to cool, oxygenate, and remove harmful gases.

Judy Tipton said she and other tournament anglers developed the simple and inexpensive ventilation system of out a desire "to keep our bass alive and healthy."

"Even though we often got through the weigh-ins without a dead fishing or penalty, it was obvious the health of our fish had greatly declined and the prospect of survival was low once we released them," she explained.

Tipton recalled an August tournament on Barren River Lake. "The release area had hundreds of dead fishing floating," she said. "Anglers were knee deep in the water, attempting to resuscitate struggling fish, and some just poured out their fish, turned their backs and walked away.

"It was horrible. I remember thinking I was ashamed to be a part of this. As much as I love fishing and competing in tournaments, I was not proud to be a tournament angler that day."

Realizing there had to be a better way, she and her associates developed the V-T2. They recognized that a closed livewell system creates water-quality problems by holding heat and harmful gases and limiting dissolved oxygen.

"Aerators are great and needed," Tipton said. "But to save on battery power they usually run on a timer. Fish need continuous oxygen flow the entire time they're in the livewell.

"Interval aeration creates a roller coaster of oxygen levels and a very unstable and more stressful environment."

By opening up the livewell to the atmosphere, the V-T2 utilizes natural processes to cool, oxygenate, and remove harmful gases. Wind and boat movement enhance the benefits.

---

33. What I Learned from Sam Griffin

*A*uthor's note: Born on a houseboat in Clewiston, Fla., in 1937, Sam Griffin carved his first topwater bait from guava wood when he was 15. It sank. But he kept trying, as he worked as a guide for his father's business, Uncle Joe's Fish Camp on Lake Okeechobee.

Today, he makes several types of topwater lures from red and white cedar, including my favorites, the Lil' Richard, a dynamite twitch bait that attracts largemouths and smallmouths alike, and the Offset Sam, a slush bait that can generate tremendous blowups at almost any time of day.

The legendary Sam Griffin

Sam doesn't turn out as many lures as he used to, and he's retired from guiding. But the man who probably knows more about Lake Okeechobee and its history than any other, is still kind enough to take me fishing annually. As we fish he shares his knowledge of and love for this natural treasure, as well as the decades of knowledge he accumulated about topwater fishing specifically and bass fishing generally.

"I love it as much today as when I was 12 and the customers had to crank the boat engine for me," he says.

In his own words, here is just a sampling of what I have learned from my friend Sam Griffin:

*   *   *   *

1. Your first fish on topwater is like your first kiss. You never forget it.

2. If you knew everything, you'd quit fishing because there's no challenge in it. Every time you go fishing, you think "I'm going to figure this out." But if you did, you wouldn't like that, although you keep trying. That's human nature. Sometimes you do figure it out, for a given day.

3. Tough fishing separates the men from the boys. That's when you have to entice them.

4. If you're going to get lost you want to have a full tank of gas. As long as you have gas, you're never lost.

5. When going into a backwater, look behind so you can see what it looks like when you want to go out.

6. I retie every six months, whether I need to or not.

7. An awful lot of fish are caught on topwater baits (in tournaments), and the angler will not tell people what he is doing. He's going to try to keep it a secret. The way the secret gets out is from his co-angler.

8. Patience and slow fishing will catch a lot more fish than fishing fast. I tell people they have to learn to catch more

fish rather than make more casts. Be superhumanly patient, and not just when fishing.

9. Back when we used to keep fish, I never found wild shiners in a fish unless it was caught on one. More bass eat small to medium baitfish than large baitfish.

10. If you want to get a bite, just look away for a second.

11. Pads shade out hydrilla and provide spawning areas for bass.

12. In the winter, big fish like to get into hydrilla because it retains heat. That's their jackets, their blankets, their heating pads. They're not foraging for food so you have to catch them by flipping, which is more of a reactionary bite.

13. From November to April, the number of large bass in the grass doubles. They're coming in to spawn.

14. I don't like hydrilla. It's a mud builder and interferes with the spawning cycle. We caught a lot of bass in Okeechobee before it was there.

15. Fish like boat trails (through vegetation). Current flow is generated by wind and that can generate a good bite as well as help keep the bottom clean so grasses like hydrilla won't take over.

16. Fish move up and down on slopes. A faster taper holds more fish.

17. For the last ten feet to the boat, look at your bait! Watch what's going on in the water when you lift it out. That will help tell you what the fish want.

18. When you're retrieving a surface lure to make another cast, hold the rod tip up, with the line going straight down to the plug. If you hold the rod down the lure will turn over and over and twist the line. A kinked line is bad to pick up the front hook on a topwater lure.

19. I recommend monofilament for topwater fishing because it's stiffer. Braided line is limp and gets tangled in the front hook. You can eliminate that by tying a rubber band on braided line in two granny knots. Do a series of about four over 2 inches. That will stiffen up the braid and that helps. It looks ugly, but doesn't take away from the fishing.

20. On a topwater bait you want as big a hook as possible that won't interfere with the action. The belly hook is important (for catching bass), while the tail hook is to make the bait float right.

21. If the water gets cold enough in Florida, you need to go play golf and not go fishing, or go to Disney World. The fishing gets really tough down here when it's cold.

PART FIVE: All in the Family: The Other Bass

---

34. No. 1 for a Reason

*I*ts aggressiveness alone makes the largemouth bass deserving of its status as the No. 1 sport fish in North America.

Dr. James A. Henshall, author of *Book of the Black Bass*, solidified that reputation more than a century ago when he wrote, "I consider him (black bass), inch for inch and pound for pound, the gamest fish that swims."

Today, the largemouth's pugnacious nature and cooperative attitude fuel a multi-billion-dollar recreational fishing industry.

But that status is about more than aggressiveness and fighting ability. The largemouth— and to a lesser extent its smallmouth and spotted bass cousins—is also pervasive, with established populations in 49 of the 50 states, as well as Mexico and Canada. No other predator species come close to being as hardy and adaptable to a variety of climates and conditions.

The angler who lives more than a few hours' drive from a bass fishery is the exception rather than the rule.

But that strength has become a liability as well in recent years, as highlighted by the ongoing "war on bass" in the West, with size and creel limits removed in some Oregon and Washington waters.

"I consistently run into salmon and steelhead anglers who are willing to break out in fisticuffs over bass," said Lonnie Johnson, conservation director for the Oregon B.A.S.S. Nation. "When I attempt to reasonably and calmly explain about the science and studies, they get a glazed look in their eyes."

What's going on? Why the war?

Despite being established in 49 states, bass aren't native to the West, or New England and much of the Mid-Atlantic either, for that matter. In fact, their original range included little more than 20 states, from the Upper Midwest to Florida and over into eastern Texas.

"We don't believe largemouth bass were in Chesapeake Bay originally," said Joe Love, Tidal Bass Manager for the Maryland Department of Natural Resources. "Their range was the Great Lakes and the Mississippi and Ohio rivers. We suspect they were introduced to the Potomac and the Eastern Shore in the late 1800s. We refer to them as 'introduced' or 'non-native' species."

In the late 19th and early 20th centuries, resource managers paid little or no attention to a fish's native range as they moved bass, rainbow trout, and other species all over the country and introduced the common carp and brown trout from Europe.

"Largemouth bass were originally introduced by the Utah Division of Wildlife Resources (UDWR) in 1890, likely via railroad," said Craig Walker, Aquatics Section Assistant Chief for the UDWR.

Bass thrived almost everywhere they were stocked, including the rivers of Washington and Oregon. Trout and other species often did not. Waters across the country became even more hospitable for bass as dams were built and impoundments created during the first half of the 20th century.

Dams on the Columbia and other rivers in the Northwest were as harmful to salmon as they were beneficial to bass. With spawning migrations hindered and/or blocked, salmon numbers began to plummet, which brings us to the present day war on bass. Although studies don't support the claim, many people believe the introduced species harms native salmon because of its predation on smolts migrating downstream through the gauntlet of dams.

On the other hand, many bass fishermen believe state agencies are playing politics instead of managing the resource based on science.

"Now, of course, all bag limits on the Columbia have been removed," said Johnson. "ODFW (Oregon Department of Fish and Wildlife) has stated that although they are a science-based agency and no science says that bass are overly predating on salmon and steelhead smolts. They're making a policy change, and using regulation simplification as the reason. Washington is now taking the same approach.

"I feel this has irreparably harmed the relationship between ODFW and warmwater anglers," he continued. "I still receive e-mails, texts, and forwarded messages from anglers asking when we plan on burning down the ODFW."

But while bass anglers have a legitimate complaint about the removal of limits on bass in the Columbia and other rivers, wildlife agencies and native species advocates have just cause for concern about the irresponsible actions of "bait-bucket biologists." They illegally stock bass in waters where the bass do pose a threat to native species.

In New York, illegal introductions of largemouth and smallmouth bass have done irreparable harm to native brook trout populations in the Adirondacks. "Brook trout evolved with minimal to no competition from other fish species and do not do well when other fish are introduced," explained Ed Woltmann with the New York State Department of Environmental Conservation.

"Bucket biologists are a growing problem for us," said Utah's Walker, who added that his state is trying several approaches to minimize the problem.

"First, we're trying to address the movement of these species through outreach and messaging, highlighting the negative consequences of illegal fish movement and equating the impacts to those of human-caused catastrophic forest fires," he added.

Utah is trying to be proactive by providing fishing opportunities for anglers to make illegal stocking less likely. The state is working to develop sterile fish for stocking to minimize the impact if they're illegally moved. Utah also uses tagged fish contests to remove unwanted species where use of rotenone and other fish toxicants isn't practical.

In Oregon, the B.A.S.S. Nation is a partner in the Turn In Illegal Introductions project, which offers rewards up to $3,000 for people who report illegal stocking of bass.

"What ODFW thinks of the program is that it's meant to educate the 'bubba' warmwater anglers about moving bass around," said Johnson. "The facts are that the single most illegally introduced species in Oregon is the rainbow trout. ODFW admits it, but still feels the warmwater community needs education. This is just species bias in action."

The bottom line is that a century ago we didn't know moving fish could have a detrimental effect on native species, and that's how the largemouth bass became the nation's most widely established sport fish. Today we do know, and anglers should leave stocking to their state fisheries managers.

What's it mean?

According to the U.S. Fish and Wildlife Service (FWS), "an exotic species is any species, including its seeds, eggs, spores, or other biological material capable of propagating that species, that is not native to that habitat."

Other terms sometimes used for exotic species include "non-native," "non-indigenous," and "alien."

A native species is a species that historically occurs/occurred in a particular habitat.

In other words, bass are exotics in much of their established range today. But that doesn't necessarily mean they're invasive. "An invasive species is an exotic species whose introduction into an ecosystem in which the species is not native causes (or is likely to cause) environmental or economic harm or harm to human health," FWS said. "It's important to note that when we talk about a species being invasive, we're talking about ecosystem or environmental boundaries, not political ones."

In states where bass aren't native, wildlife agencies often classify them as "introduced" species, unless they are problematic, usually because of illegal stocking. In those cases, they are classified as "invasive."

Most popular species

A 2011 survey found the black bass was the most popular species among 27.1 million anglers who fished freshwater, other than the Great Lakes.

More than 10.6 million anglers spent 171 million days fishing for bass. Panfish were second, with 7.3 million fishing 97 million days. In the Great Lakes, walleye slightly edged out bass for the top spot.

Altogether, freshwater anglers numbered 27.5 million, fished 456 million days, and spent $25.7 billion on fishing trips and equipment.

35. The Place to Go for Big Spots

Northern California is quickly becoming for trophy spotted bass what Florida and Texas long have been for largemouths. In fact, it's nearly impossible to keep track of the number of double-digit fish coming from there during the past few years, with Bullards Bar Reservoir as Ground Zero.

Nick Dulleck caught the latest world record there, an 11-4 giant, on Valentine's Day of 2017. The previous record, also from California, came from that 4,800-acre fishery in the Sierra Nevada foothills, checking in at 10-6.

"In the past five years at Bullards Bar, record-caliber spotted bass have been caught so many times that unless you're among the fanatical few who track this type of thing, it's difficult to keep it all straight," said Tom Stienstra in the *San Francisco Chronicle*.

Anglers also reported catching 11-pound-plus spots in December 2015 and January 2016, but didn't reveal the locations.

Bullards Bar and New Melones were included with Lake McClure, Whiskeytown, and Shasta as the five fisheries that could yield "the biggest spotted bass ever," according to *California Sportsman*.

Why do spots grow so large in these lakes? They're gobbling up stocked kokanee (landlocked salmon) and trout, a tactic similar to what hefty largemouths employ in southern California lakes.

"Spotted bass in most of our reservoirs have figured out 'We don't need to care about shad balls. We don't need to come to the banks to feed. We can just eat kokanee,' and that's what they focus on," said Bub Tosh of Paycheck Baits. "They school up like yellowfin tuna. You'll stumble across a little wolf pack of giant spots and it'll stop your heart."

Kentucky vs. Alabama

Genetics is another factor these California giants have going for them. Introduced to state waters in 1974, they are Alabama spotted bass, which grow considerably larger than Kentucky (northern) spotted bass. For years scientists and record keepers lumped the two together. But in 2011, genetic evidence convinced the American Fisheries Society to recognize the Alabama as a separate species.

Outside of California, spots are found throughout the central and lower Mississippi River basin and as far south as Texas and the Florida Panhandle. Mostly they are the Kentucky strain, with the Alabama bass limited to its native range, which is the Alabama/Mobile River system, and a few other fisheries, such as Texas' Lake Alan Henry, where the Texas Parks and Wildlife Department (TPWD) introduced them in 1996.

"The habitat there looked to favor spotted bass more than largemouths," said Craig Bonds, Director of Inland Fisheries. "Deep water, steep banks, hard clay, gravel, and chunks of rock on the bottom. They have really thrived in the lake."

In Alabama the state record is 8.9375 (8 pound, 15 ounces), caught in 1978, while Alan Henry yielded a 5.98-pounder in 2016 for the Texas "Kentucky spotted bass record."

Confused?

Right now, Texas recognizes only the Kentucky spotted bass for records and regulations, and thus the Alan Henry fish owns the top spot. But TPWD has recommended differentiating between the two species. When that happens, the 5.98 will become the "Alabama bass" state record, while the "Kentucky spotted bass" record returns to a 5.56-pounder caught in 1966 at Lake O' the Pines.

Kentucky spots don't get much larger than that, with 2- to 3-pound fish being more the norm in reservoirs. Some fisheries crank out big Kentucky spots of 4 to 6 pounds, with Georgia's Allatoona, Lanier, and Carters among the most notable.

"It all depends on forage and habitat," said Gene Gilliland, B.A.S.S. National Conservation Director. "When spotted bass have plenty of forage, like blueback herring or shad, they get bigger. And they don't need vegetation the way largemouths do."

However, Kentucky spots are often problematic, especially in streams, where they rarely exceed 12 inches and become prolific, sometimes crowding out or even hybridizing with smallmouth bass. In some of these waters they were illegally or unintentionally introduced. Other times, they migrated.

"In Oklahoma, we've had no limits on spotted bass for years," said Gilliland, a former fisheries biologist in that state. "But it's almost a useless regulation and hasn't helped with harvest because people don't keep bass."

Missouri provides a perfect case history of unintentional expansion and unforeseen consequences. Once confined to lowland ditches and streams to the southeast and west of the Ozarks, Kentucky bass "went everywhere" as reservoirs were built during the mid- century, according to Jeff Koppelman, a fisheries biologist with the Missouri Department of Conservation.

Today, they're a prominent species in fisheries such as Table Rock, Bull Shoals, and Lake of the Ozarks, among others.

How did they get to Lake of the Ozarks, an impoundment on the Osage River, which is a tributary of the Missouri and geographically separate from the spot's native range?

In 1941, about 90,000 bass—largemouth, smallmouth, and spotted—were collected from streams during the low water of summer and taken to hatcheries. They were released in the fall. Possibly spotted bass were taken to and released from a hatchery in the Osage River drainage.

Additionally, spotted bass were stocked in streams north of the Missouri River in an attempt to supplement the limited fishery.

Today, spotted bass make up about 18 percent of the bass population at Lake of the Ozarks, according to electrofishing surveys. That's down considerably from 1990 and 1991, when they outnumbered largemouths. Most interesting, though, a 5-9 spotted/smallmouth hybrid was caught there in 2012, even though bronzebacks weren't thought to be in this 80-year-old impoundment.

---

36. The Rest of the Gang: Shoal, Guadalupe Bass, and Others

*I*f you think largemouths, smallmouths, and spots are the only fish worth pursuing, you don't know your bass. As the most adaptable and widespread species in the black bass family, they certainly earned fame and your loyalty. But if you enjoy catching hard-fighting fish in scenic rivers and streams, you should meet their stay-at-home cousins—most notably shoal and Guadalupe bass.

"I used to think smallmouth bass were the ultimate river bass, but shoal bass have completely changed my mind," said Steven Sammons, an avid angler as well as fisheries scientist and research fellow in Auburn University's School of Fisheries, Aquaculture, and Aquatic Sciences.

"They grow faster, consistently reach larger sizes, and may be the

Shoal bass caught by Steve Sammons

most aggressive black bass we have. I routinely fish for them with topwater lures most suited to peacock bass and they are usually up to the challenge!"

And the Guadalupe? Tim Birdsong, a fisherman who also happens to be Habitat Conservation Branch Chief for Texas Parks and Wildlife (TPW), feels much the same way about this smaller river fish.

"It fights harder than any other species I've caught," he said. "Guadalupes know how to move their bodies in current and they are inextricably linked to flowing water. They hang out just behind the current and move into it to ambush."

With such glowing recommendations, why don't more anglers know about and fish for these moving water brawlers? Unlike largemouths, smallmouths, and spots, they can't tolerate reservoir conditions, and consequently are restricted to free-flowing waters in their historic ranges. That means anglers must go to the Hill Country of central and south Texas to fish for the Guadalupe, the state's official fish, and to the Apalachicola River drainage (Chattahoochee and Flint tributary systems) in Alabama, Georgia, and Florida to fish for shoal bass.

But a little travel time is well worth it, according to Sammons, who caught three 5-pound-plus shoal bass one day this past spring.

"Those who know what they're doing—and there are many better than I—routinely catch 5-pound shoal bass every spring," he said. "The better anglers' number of fish in those sizes is in the dozens annually. Not many smallmouth rivers can produce fish like that."

Additionally, he added, they aren't difficult to catch just about any time if you're in the right place.

And where is that for the shoal bass? The "epicenter" for big shoal bass, Sammons explained, is the Flint River west of Thomaston, Georgia. "There are five or six places you can access for float trips," he said. "And you can canoe or wade fish."

The Flint River between Albany and Lake Seminole, meanwhile, can accommodate larger boats and seems to hold bigger, but fewer, fish.

In Florida, the Chipola River, especially below Marianna, offers some of the best shoal bass fishing. Fisheries biologist Andy Strickland said that three low-water years, starting in 2006, produced big year classes of shoal bass that are now moving into the 4- and 5-pound range. But Ray Tice's state record (5.2 pounds), the fourth in little more than a year, came from the Apalachicola River in Gadsden County.

Where do you find shoal bass in those rivers? "They set up like salmon or trout," Sammons explained. "They aren't behind a rock or in an eddy. "They set up in that fast water, the first big drop in a shoal. They're in front of the 'push' water."

In Texas the lower Colorado River below Austin boasts a trophy fishery for Guadalupe bass, and, in fact, that's where Bryan Townsend caught the record, 3.71 pounds, on a crawfish-pattern fly in 2014. Birdsong added that about 60 percent of anglers targeting the state fish cast flies as they wade or drift.

The Llano River, a tributary of the Colorado, is another good choice. "Around Kingsland you have a different kind of river channel with granite outcrops," Birdsong said. "It's a great area to wade fish."

Sadly, the Guadalupe is no longer found in some of its range, mostly because of development. "We see this as an urgent time to do something meaningful to protect the species," the biologist said, pointing out that population in the Hill Country has increased by one million people during the past decade.

"Fourteen species of fish are found in the Hill Country and nowhere else in the world," he added. "We're really concerned about urbanization and demand on our spring-fed rivers."

That's why TPW initiated the 10-year Guadalupe Bass Restoration Initiative in 2010, hoping a public-private conservation partnership can help sustain and/or restore the rivers.

In addition, populations of the shoal and other black bass species mentioned below seem to be slowly declining due to habitat degradation and hybridization with illegally introduced non-native bass, especially spots. That why Sammons and other fisheries scientists in state agencies and universities within their native ranges have stepped up conservation efforts.

Nine species

Generally speaking, nine species of black bass are now recognized by the scientific community: northern largemouth bass, Florida largemouth bass, Alabama spotted bass, northern spotted bass, smallmouth bass, Guadalupe bass, shoal bass, redeye bass, and Suwannee bass.

Until 1999, the shoal was considered a subspecies of the redeye, which is why the 8-12 caught in the Apalachicola River in 1995 is recognized as the all-tackle record by the International Game Fish Association, but not by Florida as a state record. The Georgia record, meanwhile, is an 8-3 caught in 1977 on the Flint River and the Alabama record is a 6-11 caught from Halawakee Creek in 1996.

Although similar in overall appearance to the shoal, the redeye is a smaller fish and prefers skinnier waters in Alabama, Georgia, South Carolina, and small portions of North Carolina and Tennessee. The Georgia state record, 3-7, came from Lake Hartwell in 2004.

"It's not found in the fast water," said Sammons. "It doesn't need boulders like the shoal. Mostly you catch them in small pools with 6-pound line and small crankbaits."

As scientific investigative methods improve and conservation efforts for native species intensify, it's possible the redeye will be subdivided into several different species in the years to come, including Coosa, Tallapoosa, Chattahoochee, Cahaba, and Warrior.

Because of its association with a song written by Steven Foster, the Suwannee bass is the most recognized black bass outside the big five. But it has the smallest range of the family—the Suwannee, Santa Fe, Wacissa, Wakulla, and several other free-flowing Florida rivers, as well as the Alapaha, Ochlockonee, and Withlacoochee shared by Florida and Georgia. The current IGFA record is 3-14, taken from the Suwannee in 1985.

During the next few years, Choctaw and the Bartram's likely will be the next bass to be recognized as separate species, Sammons said. "The genetics is really strong on the Choctaw," he explained. "It looks like a spotted bass, but it's geographically isolated." In fact, the Florida Fish and Wildlife Conservation Commission already includes the Choctaw in its fishing regulations.

The Bartram's, meanwhile, "should be a slam dunk" to be recognized, the Auburn scientist said. "It's found only in the Savannah and Broad River drainages and it's the only one (outside the big five) to survive in reservoirs. You can catch it in lakes and it gets a little bigger, 2 to 2 1/2 pounds."

ROBERT MONTGOMERY

37. The Striped Bass Debate

Some fishermen don't like striped bass. Asian carp, including the grass-eating variety, probably rank highest on the hate list. But stripers are in the top five at least, along with chemical spraying of aquatic vegetation, the animal rights movement, and threats to public access.

The only problem is that the stripers don't deserve their bad reputation. Biologists have uncovered nothing to suggest they harm bass populations through predation. The only evidence against them is anecdotal: By chance, an angler sees a striper eat a largemouth.

And that does happen. In the fish world, a large specimen will eat a smaller one if the opportunity arises, no question. Sometimes the eater and the eatee are of the same species. In other words, black bass are cannibals, as are stripers, walleye, trout, and every other predatory species.

So . . . when a fishery is in need of a supplemental stocking of bass, should we not do it because of that? Meanwhile, plenty of proof asserts that, when stocked in a reservoir, stripers do not harm the black bass fishery. Study after study reveals that shad make up about 95 percent of a striper's diet.

In fact, sometimes striped bass enhance the black bass fishery. "Stocking stripers in Lake Texoma improved both bass and crappie fisheries," said Gene Gilliland, National Conservation Director for B.A.S.S. and former fisheries biologist with the Oklahoma Department of Wildlife Conservation.

That's because the larger, open-water stripers gobbled up gizzard shad that were too big for other predators to eat. In doing so, the dynamics of the forage population shifted to one dominated by smaller fish, which both largemouths and crappie could take advantage of.

Why, then, did the Arkansas Game and Fish Commission (AGFC) decide not to join the Missouri Department of Conservation (MDC) in a multi-year program to stock stripers in Bull Shoals, a 45,000-acre border impoundment on the White River?

AGFC fisheries chief Mark Oliver cited angler opposition. "We know that the low striped bass stocking rates outlined in the proposal would not negatively impact other popular game fish such as walleye and bass," he said. "But we didn't receive an abundance of support for the proposal."

Why was that? Gilliland theorizes it might be due to "circumstantial evidence." Arkansas anglers saw stripers stocked in another fishery and caught fewer bass afterward. "They think there's a cause and effect, but the decline is related to something else," he explained. "Lakes all over the country have stripers and bass and they're doing just fine."

Based on more than 70 percent support for the plan shown at four joint public meetings, Missouri elected to go ahead with the plan to stock at a low rate every other year. Many of the fish will take up residence in Arkansas, where most of the lake lies.

"We stock stripers in Lake of the Ozarks and continue to have good bass fishing there," said MDC's A.J. Pratt. "In fact, it's a phenomenal largemouth fishery."

The Missouri biologist added 16,000 stripers every other year "is a drop in the bucket, but if we see it's having an impact (on the bass population), we'll adjust the stocking."

In rare cases, too many stripers have been stocked in a fishery with a limited food supply and both stripers and bass suffered from slow growth rates as a result. That's not likely in this reservoir with an abundance of shad.

Because it's a flood control reservoir with fluctuating water levels, Bull Shoals doesn't get consistent bass recruitment, meaning the quality of the bass fishery is cyclical, Pratt said. Adding stripers at low densities will offer anglers an enhanced opportunity to catch fish during lows in the cycle, as was the case with the introduction of walleye.

So, even though some people don't want them, Arkansas fishermen, along with those from Missouri, now have another fish to catch. Many will enjoy doing so; others will not—and they'll have a new excuse to use when they don't catch bass.

38. What I Learned at the Bassmaster Classic

*A*t my first Bassmaster Classic, press and pros had dinner one night at the Playboy Club in Cincinnati. Bunny Jennifer looked great in black. We left with souvenir photos and books of matches. Later on, I think some guys actually went fishing.

At my next, we had dinner on the governor's lawn in Little Rock. I sat at the same table with then Gov. Bill Clinton and B.A.S.S. founder Ray Scott. Both of those guys could have made a fortune selling used cars.

Back then, Classics were staged during late summer when days on the water typically were hot, humid, and miserable. But a hurricane moved north from the Gulf of Mexico during the practice days for that Arkansas Classic so it wasn't quite as hot. But an unrelenting downpour made conditions even more miserable.

As an incentive to get up at 3:30 a.m. and ride with the pros as observers, B.A.S.S. offered $500 to the journalist who caught the biggest bass each day, as well as his partner. Paired with Lonnie Stanley, I spent the second practice day huddled in my leaky rainsuit, dangling a Cordell Spot lipless crankbait behind the boat. The current vibrated the bait so I didn't have to cast.

Although it didn't occur to me until later, Lonnie didn't catch a fish that day. But about an hour before we were to go in, a small spotted bass hit my bait. I boated it, unhooked it, and started to throw it back.

"Wait a minute," Lonnie said. "That could be the biggest fish of the day."

I held it up and gazed critically at it through the pounding rain. "Really?" I said. "This?"

He nodded. "Fishing's tough. Keep it."

We were the last of 40 or so boats to be driven into the coliseum for the practice weigh-in. As we pulled up to the stage, the announcer noted that the largest bass thus far weighed 1 pound, 7 ounces. Mine weighed 1 pound, 8 ounces. Lonnie and I each pocketed $500.

And the lipless crankbait has been my go-to confidence bait ever since. No matter where I'm going to fish, or for what species, I carry several with me. I don't particularly like throwing the bait. But if the fishing is slow, I tie it on, and, more times than not, it produces.

I can give you all kinds of logical reasons for that. For example, I'm making more casts and covering more water. Or I'm provoking dormant fish to instinctively strike.

But I think it's just as much about attitude as about the bait itself and how it performs in the water. No matter how tough the fishing, I feel confident the lipless crankbait will produce for me, as it did during that torrential tropical storm on the Arkansas River.

Here's what else I learned at the Bassmaster Classic:

1. Mr. DeMille, I'm ready for my close up.

Most of the early pros started out as fishing guides. Behind the scenes they sometimes grumbled a bit about the cost they paid in loss of privacy for becoming professionals and fishing for big prizes. Overeager fans followed too close in their own boats. And with someone watching at nearly all times, heeding nature's call became difficult. The year Guido Hibdon won the Classic, I fished with him on a day that was particularly painful for both of us. He complained. I sympathized.

But one man in particular embraced it. As the camera boat zoomed toward us on a practice day, Roland Martin put down his fishing rod and pulled a comb and mirror from the glove box. Thus, I wasn't surprised that he parlayed his success as a bass pro into a TV career, hosting "Fishing with Roland Martin."

2. Mighty Casey has struck out.

Rick Clunn, who earned a berth in the Classic more than 30 times and won it four, had the lead going into the last day and I was paired with him. He fished long and hard, yet failed to put a keeper in the boat. He wouldn't win a fifth this day. He didn't say a half dozen words all day, and I suspected disappointment and/ or anger would keep him from saying anything as we waited in the hot, August sun to be towed back to the amphitheater. I was wrong.

"Hey, it happens to everyone," he said. And then, when a passing competitor asked how he had done, he responded with "I got a limit" to have a little fun with his failure.

3. Aim small. Miss small.

That was the shooting advice Frank Martin gave his sons in the movie *The Patriot*. At the Classic, I learned that applies to fishing too. Those who qualify for the Classic aren't just the world's best bass fishermen. They're also the best casters. They don't throw to an area; they hit specific spots. And they do so consistently, placing their baits in locations many of us never could reach. That skill helps elevate them above the rest. If you want to catch more and bigger fish, practice your casting.

4. Know your opponent.

During one Classic, I fished with a pro on his "home water." The pressure he felt was clearly evident as he sped from place to place, made a few casts, and moved some more. At the same time he often voiced concerns about how the other contenders were doing. He didn't fare well that day or in the tournament.

But also I fished with many who won. Almost to a man, they didn't worry about what other anglers were doing. They were just out fishing, much the same as they would be if they weren't participating in the world's most prestigious bass tournament. They focused on the fish and what they must do to catch them.

PART SIX: Your Tackle Box

---

39. Top Secrets

*I*ts rubber skirt long ago dried up and crumbled into dust, but the old yellow Hula Popper remains one of my most prized possessions. I haven't fished with it in 40 years and, as best I can remember, I caught only one bass with it.

But that one fish . . . well, it set the course I followed as a lifelong angler, including friendship with Sam Griffin, a lure designer and one of the world's best topwater fishermen. That's why I so love that Hula Popper.

Yet, I didn't make the connection between that lure and my addiction to topwater fishing until I wrote an essay in my book, *Why We Fish*.

As I started to write "The Proof Is in the Popper," my intent was to point out that pleasant memories of previous trips are some of the main reasons we fish. But then the essay took on a life of its own as I visualized that fall day on Turner's pond so many years ago.

The water was flat calm and I knew next to nothing about fishing a topwater. Since the bait was a "popper," I popped it. In

The author with Sam Griffin

fact, I popped it as hard as I possibly could, sending ripples all across that pond.

As the pond returned to glasslike following my second pop, water under the lure exploded, and I was suddenly tied fast to the biggest bass I'd ever hooked.

Of course it wasn't large enough to pull drag on my Johnson Century spincast reel. But at 3 pounds, it was a trophy in my eyes as I dragged it up on the bank. My heart nearly leaped out of my chest at the sight of that fish, and, after I put it on my rope stringer, I remember looking down to see my hands still shaking.

In the decades since I've caught thousands of bass larger than the one I caught that fall day, including several that weighed 10 pounds or more. And I caught some of those lunkers on Sam's wooden surface baits, mostly the Offset Sam.

But I've never caught one that excited me more than that 3-pounder did. And as I wrote about it, I suddenly realized, hey, that's why I like topwater so much!

How can a 3-pounder I caught on top as a child mean more to me than 10-pounders I've caught as an adult?

If you've ever returned to the elementary school where you went to as a child, you know the halls, rooms, desks, and everything else look smaller than in your memories. Well, it's the same thing with fishing.

I have no doubt that if a 3-pound bass were to blow up on that Hula Popper today in exactly the same way as that one from my childhood, the explosion would pale in comparison to what I remember.

But just as school is larger in our memories than in the reality of adulthood, so too is that strike. That's why I'd rather throw a topwater than anything else. I remember how that blowup excited me and I want more, in much the same way that an addict needs his fix.

And that's why I'm so blessed to have Sam as a friend. It's as if some higher power led the student to his teacher. For years, Sam made baits for Luhr Jensen, including the Jerk'n Sam. Now he makes his own line, including the Offset Sam, a slush bait, and the Lil' Richard, a finesse lure that has been his biggest seller.

"Keep throwing a topwater and eventually you will get bit," says the man who's been designing and making topwater lures for more nearly four decades and who has lived on and fished on Lake Okeechobee for most of his 80-plus years. While guiding and "field testing" his lures, he has logged more time on the water than almost any professional bass fisherman.

Sam's advice

"Patience and persistence are the keys. Slow yourself and your retrieve down. It's not the number of casts you make in a day, but the placement of your lure and the attention you give your lure that are most important. Let the fish help you determine the best method.

"After the lure impacts the water, watch it and the area around it for signs of movement. If you see action, but the cast doesn't produce a strike, try again in the same area. Continue casting until you think there isn't any interest from the fish.

"A wake behind the lure usually means you're working it too fast, or maybe the fish just doesn't have enough interest to strike. Work the lure slower for a few more casts. Then, if the bass still doesn't strike, change to another type of surface lure in a smaller size. If the fish still doesn't react, move on, but remember the spot and return later to give it another try.

"If the fish boils just after you remove the lure from the water, it can mean it's holding in deeper water under your boat or it may have followed the lure out from your original target. Try moving your boat farther from the bank, grass edge, or the underwater cover you're fishing.

"Keep your mind on the job at hand. If you're thinking of anything but fishing, then you're not fishing right and you could miss bites."

Sam's tantalizing tidbits

- Topwater doesn't have to be early (or late). That's just when people used to fish because they worked during the day. Ten to two can be the best time for big fish.
- You can catch bass consistently in water that's 50 degrees or above. In colder water you usually want to fish faster or slower, not in between.

- The popper is a good choice for cold water because you can keep it in one place longer and its tail sits down in the water, making it easier for the fish to take.
- A popper is also the best bait when fish are holding tight to cover. You don't necessarily have to pop it. Just twitch it and let it sit there.
- A bass can suck the bait in like a vacuum cleaner or hit it so hard it knocks the paint off.
- Your reaction time is faster than you think, so be careful. You have to let the fish eat the bait.
- Don't set the hook hard. Just "snug" the bass. It turns sideways after it strikes.
- I use at least 15-pound line. Lighter than that goes limp and gets tangled on the hooks.
- For 85 to 90 percent of my retrieves I use the same cadence, two jerks and let it sit. I let the fish dictate how hard to jerk.
- You want to use a faster retrieve in rough water to take the slack out of the line.
- A bass will hit sometimes just to kill the bait. That's the predator part of the brain. It's being mean, just like a junk yard dog. You want to "feel" the fish before you set the hook.
- Eighty five percent of my bites come when the bait is still or coming to a stop.
- The size of the lure is more important than the color.
- I use black and white (topwater baits) 75 percent of the time. And, personally, I think a little red under the nose and tail helps. Most of those color choices are just a "between the ears" thing. Usually, it's the action, not the color.
- Mylar tinsel on the back hook gets me 25 percent more bites. Glitter on the sides (of bait) gets their attention from farther away.

- The same bait will catch fish anywhere. It's a matter of confidence. That's why there are regional favorites.
- Throw to anything different, like where two different types of grasses meet. Where pepper grass meets bulrushes is the best. Also, throw in the holes.

A catch with the Lil' Richard lure

---

40. The Line on Stretch

*A*s a bass fisherman, you've read or heard about line stretch. You've noted the pros and fishing industry experts say it isn't good to use monofilament in some applications because of that stretch. But do you really believe them? Have they convinced you that braid is the best line for some methods?

Or is it all just hype?

Like many, perhaps you think mono works fine for you and you see no reason to complicate your fishing with another type of line that's often more expensive. So what if your mono line stretches a bit? It's not breaking on you. You catch fish. How bad could it be?

Tournament angler and lure designer Troy Gibson had his doubts too. But after testing the stretch properties of mono, copolymer, fluorocarbon, and braid for himself, he doesn't anymore.

A catch with braided line

"Oh, my gosh, was I surprised at what I learned," he said. "After I did this and switched to braid (for some applications), my hookup rate went way up. I was able to transform all my setting energy from the rod into the bait. I've hooked more bites and I've caught more fish."

And now that he's a convert, Gibson also is a vocal disciple. "Other anglers really need to try this too, to see for themselves," he said.

His recommendation: Tie a 20-foot length of line to a pole or wall. Attach a pencil to the other end. Then pull the line out as straight as possible, without stretching it, and make a mark on the ground or floor.

Now stretch the line as much as you can and mark that spot as well.

"Once you do this, you'll understand about line stretch," he said. "It will open your mind and make you a better fisherman. "Line companies are really missing out by not doing a better job of putting out this information."

What Gibson discovered is that mono typically stretches 1 inch per foot, copolymer ½ inch, and fluorocarbon ¼. Braid, of course, doesn't stretch.

To put that discovery into angling context, imagine you've made a 20-yard cast with mono and a bass strikes the bait before you begin a retrieve. That means your line will stretch 60 inches—five feet—as you set the hook. That translates into both lost speed and power.

And lost fish.

"When a bass chomps down on a bait and closes its mouth, your hook is not going to penetrate if you have too much line stretch," said Kent Kelly, a member of Arkansas' Jonesboro Bass Club. "But when they lose that fish, most people don't equate it with line stretch."

According to Kelly, another way to see for yourself about stretch is to tie mono to a full milk jug, back up about 10 yards or so, and then try to turn over the jug with a hookset. "You won't even shake the jug with less than 20- or 25-pound test," he said. "This really opens people's eyes when they try it."

There's more. Mono has even more stretch than informal field tests reveal, according to a fishing line expert at Pure Fishing (Berkley).

Reflective of the industry, Berkley's series of monofilaments have an "ultimate elongation" of anywhere from 18 to 30 percent. That means a 20-yard piece of mono can stretch from 3.6 to 6 yards before it breaks.

"It's like you're pulling on a rubber band," said a product manager for Power Pro. "You stretch and stretch and stretch, until finally it pulls back. At first, you're just pulling on the line, and then, finally, you have the hookset."

Additionally, he explained, line stretch equates to reduced tensile (pound test) strength and abrasion resistance as well. That's because the diameter of the line diminishes.

All of this is *not* to say monofilament is inherently a bad fishing line. Rather, he's saying it isn't the best line for some methods. "Mono has plenty of applications," the Power Pro source said. "With crankbaits, it's good to have some stretch and give in your line. And it's the same with topwater."

The Pure Fishing spokesman added, "Mono gives a great cushion, especially for weekend anglers who might not have their drags set properly or use rods that are really stiff."

But today's braid is much better for specific applications and some anglers are even using it fulltime, especially in saltwater.

For bass anglers, heavy cover is one of the best places to use braid. With mono you lose pulling power and that gives the fish an advantage to stay stuck in the vegetation. With braid, you're driving the hook home and moving that fish out at the same time. Also with braid, you can keep constant pressure on the fish because the line actually cuts through the grass.

If he's using mono to throw a jig or frog in grass, Gibson said, an angler "just can't stick that fish. All it will feel is a little nudge.

"A lot of times, you think you've stuck a fish and it's coming to the boat. But when it gets close, it comes unbuttoned. Well, that fish wasn't hooked at all. It just opened its mouth and the bait came flying back at you, along with the sinker," he explained.

Even in open water, braid can produce better than mono if long casts are required to reach the fish. But braid, because it doesn't stretch, does require some adjustment, like loosening the drag or going to a softer rod.

"Beginning users pull a lot of hooks out of fish," the Power Pro spokesman said. "That's because braid doesn't have the little lag time that comes with mono. With braid you sometimes need to hesitate a fraction of a second on the hookset. "But once you understand how to use it, braid can make all of the difference in the world."

Braid today

Since it first came on the market in the 1990s, braided line has improved dramatically. "Early braid was rough and would stack on a reel," said the Power Pro source. "It would bury itself (on hookset, causing line to break) and would groove guides. "And if you got a backlash, good luck getting it out.

"Today, braid is rounder, smoother, and stacks tighter."

Pure Fishing's spokesman added, "We're using different constructions to make braid smoother. We have better fiber for improved tensile strength. And we improved coatings so the color lasts longer.

"We've even learned to make braid translucent (Fireline Crystal)."

41. The Forgotten Color

Chances are good that chartreuse is a primary color in your tackle box. It's a standard for spinnerbaits. As a dip, it sweetens the tails of soft plastics. On crankbaits and topwaters it brightens bellies and sides, as do lime, citrus, parrot, and a palette of other variations that evolved from chartreuse.

But where's the color that started it all? Where's the respect? In other words, what about school-bus yellow? Unless you carry some of the retro baits, such as the Heddon Lucky 13 and Arbogast Hula Popper, it's probably not in your box.

"Chartreuse is brighter and yellow has been forgotten," said Stephen Headrick, a lure designer and owner of Punisher Lures and Dale Hollow 1 Stop near Dale Hollow. "Yellow is now one of the most under-fished colors. But it can be a great color year around."

School-bus yellow can be especially useful during winter, when adorning an aspirin-head hair jig, also known around Dale Hollow as a "hoss fly." Those who discovered its effectiveness on smallmouth bass try to share the wealth from time to time. But they've discovered many anglers just won't believe a bait that seems designed for crappie will catch big bronzebacks.

"I've given seminars on the school-bus yellow jig and people will just not believe me," said David Duvall, a part-time guide and Dale Hollow regular.

Aside from the color, the fact that advocates recommend fishing the jig without a trailer makes the technique seem even more like a tall tale.

"People think I must be putting minnows on the jig, but I'm not," Duvall continued. "The school-bus yellow jig is just the best wintertime bait you can have for smallmouth bass, especially on clear-water lakes like Dale Hollow."

What makes this bait so effective? The hair that appears dark yellow out of water turns lighter as it sinks below 10 feet or so, explained Headrick, who makes the jigs in a variety of sizes. When water temperature falls below 55 degrees, crawfish turn a similar shade.

"You pop that lure off the bottom and it looks like a crawfish," he added. "Smallmouth bass can't resist it."

And it's not just in Dale Hollow this little appreciated bait is effective. It works in just about any lake or impoundment that has smallmouths, according to Duvall, who also has used the jig on Tim's Ford and Center Hill.

The key is to fish it in the right places. "I like flats, humps, and long gravel points," he revealed.

"Personally, I like black shale rock," added Headrick. "But any place holding crawfish can be good. Depth will depend on the weather.

"If you have clouds and wind, the fish could be in 10 feet. If it's slick and sunny, they could be 20 to 30 or even more."

Headrick's favorite size is 3/16-ounce, but he will switch to 1/8 for shallower water or ¼ in high winds. Duvall also prefers 3/16.

"I'll make a long cast, close the bail with my hand, and watch the line as it sinks," he said. "Many times, you won't feel the bite. You'll just see a slight movement of the line."

Once the jig hits bottom, Headrick advises holding the rod at a 60-degree angle for the retrieve. "Give it two quick, little jerks and let it fall back," he said. "And watch the line."

If you can't provoke a reaction strike, he continued, then try dragging the jig on bottom.

Headrick first learned about the hoss fly from his father, but smallmouth legend Billy Westmoreland is the one who convinced him of its effectiveness nearly 20 years ago. "I was using the float-n-fly and he kicked my butt with the school-bus yellow jig," he remembered.

"Outside this area, I don't think he ever told anyone about it. But he always had lots of yellow jigs with him."

Other yellow options

The aspirin-head jig seems to be the best yellow bait to throw for smallmouth bass when water temperature is in the low 50s or below. But as the water warms, other options come into play.

"Bandit has a Spring Craw crankbait that's about 75 percent school-bus yellow," said smallmouth-expert Stephen Headrick. "It's a killer in spring around mud flats, when crawfish are starting to come out and move around.

"Crawfish start spawning at about 60 degree, earlier than most believe."

A little later in the year, floating yellow worms fished straight with a wire hook will take both smallmouths and largemouths when worked around grass.

"Using yellow at that time of year has nothing to do with the water temperature, the way it does in winter," he said. "It works then because yellow is just a good color."

---

42. Hookset Advice from KVD

You will catch more bass if you set the hook properly. Many anglers mistakenly use the same "hard jerk" set for all baits, instead of just Texas-rig soft plastics.

I asked Kevin VanDam, one of the nation's top bass anglers, to tell me how he sets hooks and keep it simple. The information was for an article I wrote for children. But just about any bass fisherman can benefit from Kevin's experience.

Texas-rig soft plastics: "You have to drive the hook through the plastic," he says. "I like a little slack line. I drop the rod tip and hit real hard."

Spinnerbaits: "It's more of a pull set. Let the rod load up and pull into the fish. Reel hard and pull."

Topwaters: "Reel until you feel the weight of the fish and then set the hook. Today's (treble) hooks are so good, so sharp, that you don't need to set the hook hard."

Crankbaits: "Reel and pull."

Light-tackle spinning gear: "I don't jerk at all. I reel set. I reel fast and let the rod load up before I pull. I fish for smallmouths a lot with a spin rod. If I miss a bite, I let the rod back down and smallmouth bass will hit it (bait) again."

Braided line: "You don't need to jerk nearly as hard. That's important to remember because there's no give there. (By contrast, monofilament line stretches.) With braided line you want a shock absorber, like a softer rod tip. I use it for certain applications only."

43. The Book on Coloring

*L*ure color might play a role that most bass anglers hadn't considered, according to researchers at Ontario's Carleton University.

Lure color does not significantly affect the number of fish caught or whether hooking-related injuries are sustained, they revealed. But the right color choice could make the difference in whether you catch a 1-pound bass or a 5-pounder.

"Bright colors appeared to selectively capture larger fish than either dark or natural lure colors . . . ," they said in a report entitled "Does Lure Color Influence Catch Per Unit Effort (CPUE), Fish Capture Size, and Hooking Injury in Angled Largemouth Bass?"

"Our study reveals that while different lure colors might capture the imagination and wallet of the angler, they do not influence CPUE (catch per unit effort) or hooking injury in bass, but appear to have a small influence on the size of captured fish."

In an experiment on Lake Opinicon, a popular bass fishery, they tested six different colors of worms: leech black and bream blue (dark), natural cigar red and wasp (natural), and sherbet orange and pearl white (bright). During July and August, the baits "were fished quite passively" by anglers with intermediate skill, who caught a total of 119 bass.

Each color was fished for 20-minute intervals, and each angler fished all six before repeating a color. Bass were caught all over the lake, with a special focus on shoreline areas.

Blue caught the most bass, with 25, followed by black 23, white 22, wasp 17, orange 16, and red 16.

"When lure color was grouped into the dark, natural, and bright categories, there was a significant relationship detected between the color categories and the total length in millimeters of captured fish," the scientists said. "The bright lure color category caught fish that were significantly longer (mean total length of 349 mm) than fish captured on the dark (318 mm) and natural (318 mm) color categories."

Based on those findings, they concluded, "It is unlikely there is any management value in regulating lure color. Nonetheless, we expect anglers will continue to experiment with different colors of lures in their quest for the most and biggest fish."

---

44. Disappearing Act

*A*uthor's note: Saltwater captains long have favored fluorocarbon as a leader material. In the past it was too expensive for most anglers to use to fill their reels, even those with small-line capacity. That is no longer the case, as many companies have made it affordable.

*   *   *   *   *

Fluorocarbon line isn't an option for many anglers anymore.

It's a necessity.

"I used to use it about ten percent of the time," said Cliff Pace, an Elite Series angler from Mississippi. "Now I use it about 85 percent of the time."

Lake Lanier guide Mike Bucca added, "At first, I used fluorocarbon on spinning reels for finesse applications. Now that things have advanced, I use fluorocarbon about 90 percent of the time for all applications, except float-and-fly and big swimbaits."

Since fluorocarbon became available as a fishing line more than 15 years ago, this attitude change is primarily linked to product improvement. Price reduction also played a role in its increased popularity, but enhanced quality elevated fluorocarbon to nearly equal status with monofilament as the line most often used.

Many anglers who first filled their spools with fluorocarbon found it brittle, with too much memory and poor knot strength, especially in strengths of 10-pound test and higher.

"Back several years ago, you could feel the inconsistencies in fluorocarbon," said Bucca, an advocate of the Trik Fish brand. "But now I've noticed more companies are getting better at producing a smoother line. By that I mean if you run your hands up and down the line, it's very smooth, with a diameter more consistently round."

Today's fluorocarbon is "much, much better than the original," added a spokesman for Pure Fishing.

"With Berkley Vanish, we've made six (formulation) improvements. It's still thin and still at a good price, but we worked hard to make it more flexible and have better impact strength."

At Trik Fish, several reformulations made today's fluorocarbon line "relaxed and very manageable," said Dave Burkhardt, company owner. "It's mindless on the spool. You can focus on fishing and not on the line.

"I've kept fluorocarbon up to 18 months on a reel without using it," he added. "Then when I started fishing with it again, it worked great by the fifth or sixth cast. Memory had been the curse of some brands of early fluorocarbon, but, thanks to new technology, it's not a problem for us."

Today's Trik Fish fluorocarbon also has seven percent smaller diameter than premium monofilament, Burkhardt said.

Competition has been a key to the improvements in fluorocarbon, according to Pace. "At first there were just two or three brands," he said. "But now just about every company has one, and they needed to step up and make their products stand out."

While fluorocarbon has improved in terms of manageability, strength, and consistency, it still possesses the qualities that made it attractive in the first place:

- Because of its refractive ability, fluorocarbon nearly disappears in water.
- It's denser than monofilament, meaning it sinks faster and is more sensitive.
- Fluorocarbon is more resistant to degradation by ultraviolet light.
- It doesn't absorb water and has less stretch, allowing for a quicker and more efficient hookset than with monofilament.

As more and more anglers recognize these benefits and discover the old criticisms don't apply anymore, companies are increasing the variety of their offerings to take advantage of fluorocarbon's heightened popularity. For example, Trik Fish now offers spools of 600 yards, as well as 200.

"With the 200-yard spools, you'd inevitably have some waste," Burkhardt said. "With the mini-bulks, you can fill 6 to 10 reels, depending on the pound test, with little or no waste."

Berkley, meanwhile, offers "professional grade" Trilene 100% Fluorocarbon, as well as traditional Vanish.

"The 100% was our big breakthrough for the bass market about 10 years ago," the Berkley representative said. "We had never called our fluorocarbon Trilene. But once we had a line that met all the vigors, we decided we could brand it that way. It's more expensive because it is made with a special resin. Hank Parker said he thinks it's the best line in the world."

Other people like Hi-Seas Quattro Fluorocarbon with four-color camouflage. "It's softer and more manageable, and with the camo, it's more invisible," one tournament angler said.

For the Quattro, Hi-Seas figured out "how to add camo color and heighten sensitivity and softness," said a spokesman.

"Fluorocarbon is not 100 percent invisible," he added. "The camo acts as a stopper to light that travels down the line. If a fish sees that light, it doesn't see a solid piece of line because the pattern breaks it up." The colors don't interfere with the refractive ability of fluorocarbon, he added.

These options are a long way from the fluorocarbon line of 15 years ago. Back then, near invisibility was its chief selling point. It entered the freshwater market as an alternative to monofilament, braid, and copolymer when companies finally found a way to produce it at a reasonable cost. Before that, it was used exclusively as leader material, mostly in saltwater.

"There's still a learning curve for anglers with fluorocarbon," the Berkley spokesman cautioned. "For example, you want to wet your knots and tie them slowly. Fluorocarbon is sensitive to friction. On the positive side, I've heard the pros say they retie less often."

Versatility

With fluorocarbon so popular for so many applications today, it's easier to point out when it's not the best line choice, as opposed to when it is.

"Because fluorocarbon is denser and sinks faster, it's not really good for topwaters," said the Berkley rep. "And braid is probably better for flipping because it's stronger and invisibility isn't important."

Trik Fish's Dave Burkhardt added, "If you're fishing emergent vegetation with a soft jerkbait, your bait won't be as buoyant with fluorocarbon and you'll sink into the grass more."

Depending on conditions, though, a topwater and fluorocarbon can work well together. "When I am chasing schoolers I like to use fluorocarbon because I'm making long casts and working the bait rather quickly on top," said Georgia guide Mike Bucca. "Because I have less stretch, I'm able to catch more fish at the end of a long cast."

But he warns against using fluorocarbon with plus-sized lures, such as 4-ounce swimbaits. "When you're throwing big baits there's a lot of torque at the knot and mono is better at taking this excessive abuse," he said.

With just about everything else, fluorocarbon works well, although some anglers might prefer other lines for a variety of reasons.

"I feel it's advantageous to use fluorocarbon on diving lures, like jerkbaits and crankbaits," said Bucca. "Fluorocarbon is denser, which allows it to sink faster than mono. You get more depth out of your bait."

Pro Cliff Pace likes the quicker fall for weightless soft baits, such as Senkos. "It (fluorocarbon) keeps you in better contact with the bait and it's a more natural presentation," he said.

"Also, if you're fishing by a dock, the fluorocarbon lets you keep the bait close. With mono, the bait might be six or seven feet from the dock by the time it reaches bottom."

Bucca also likes to throw soft plastics with fluorocarbon, especially when he's fishing for spotted bass around rocks. He admits braid is better for sheer strength and sensitivity. But fluorocarbon offers better abrasion resistance than mono, and it's near invisibility is a decided advantage over both braid and mono.

Most recently, anglers are using fluorocarbon as an alternative to braid when flipping. They too like it because it's tough and because it "disappears" in the water. That can make it especially effective on bright days.

"I like to use the 20- or 25-pound test Trik Fish when I have to fish slower and they're looking at the bait longer," said Florida tournament angler Uby Rosell. "Bass are more likely to see the braid than the fluorocarbon."

Rosell added that he uses the 15 for flipping and pitching to grass edges with a smaller bait. "Also, I'm a co-angler," he said. "While the guys up front are using braid, I'm using fluorocarbon to get the bites they miss, especially when the fish are sensitive."

The bottom line

Fluorocarbon is made of polyvinalidene fluoride, more commonly known as PVDF, a specialty plastic material in the fluoropolymer family. PVDF can be injected, molded, and welded, and is commonly used in the chemical, semiconductor, medical, and defense industries, as well as in lithium ion batteries. It often is used as insulation on electrical wires.

45. Going Soft on Swimbaits

*A*uthor's note: For years, most anglers ignored swimbaits, leaving them for a few California stalwarts who used them to catch big bass in clear water. But then, someone discovered they were effective all over the country. As often happens in bass fishing, innovation followed. Today we have a seemingly endless array of swimbait options in a variety of shapes, sizes, and price points. My favorite, however, remains the inexpensive, soft plastic swimbait, with a weedless single hook. Perhaps that's related to the fact that I caught an 8-pound, 8-ounce largemouth the first day I tried it.

*　　*　　*　　*　　*

On Lake Okeechobee, luremaker and former guide Sam Griffin rarely throws anything besides one of his own wooden topwaters. More and more, however, he's making an exception for a hybrid bait that locals call "swimming worms."

"I'm a surface fisherman, but I've never gotten into frogs," he said. "But I've used soft plastics, and what I like about the swimming worm is that it can be a sight bait, like a surface plug. You can cover an awful lot of water with it, and they (bass) will try to destroy it."

"Florida has been one of the hottest places for this bait. People like to throw it in the grass," added Troy Gibson, tournament angler and lure designer. "But you can use it anywhere. It's universal.

"Up at Lake of the Ozarks (Missouri), you could swim it through trees and catch fish. It's just that no one has tried it yet."

But someone will soon, as word spreads about this versatile lure that seems a cross between a swimbait and a worm or soft jerkbait, and more lure companies tap into the hot market. Typically four to five inches long, these baits feature "boot" or swimbait tails. Some, such as the Skinny Dipper, are more bulky, while others, including the Swim Senko, offer a more slender profile.

"Sometimes the fish want a smaller presentation," Griffin explained. "The thinner baits are good for kids and aspiring fishermen too because they are more forgiving. Often times, the fish will hook itself."

Belly slits allow for easier Texas-style rigging on the thicker baits, while groves on top provide lower profiles for hook barbs and help keep them weedless. Also offering less bulk, paddle tail worms, including Zoom's Speed Worm and Bass Pro Shops' Paddle Stik, are popular variations of these baits.

Both types of tail impart an enticing swimming motion. But with the paddle version you should rig the bait so the tail swims left to right, instead of up and down, Gibson cautioned.

"If it's going up and down like a dolphin's tail, then it will drag through the grass," he said. "Going left to right, it makes a thumping sound so fish know it's coming and you get a reaction bite."

Griffin prefers to throw both boot and paddle tails on top, especially in and around grass. But Walt Reynolds, an Okeechobee regular and former tournament pro, agrees with Gibson regarding their versatility.

"You can fish this bait like a worm," he said. "Or you can fish it like a swimbait, using a slow retrieve in open water."

Griffin revealed that he started throwing the soft plastic swimbaits when water was low on Okeechobee. "We were swimming it over rocks," he said. "It was an open-water bait then."

In a nutshell, these are "action baits that you can rip and pull," Gibson said. "I think that's why they're so popular.

"They're becoming a replacement for spinnerbaits. Fish have seen so many spinnerbaits over the years, but they haven't seen this. You can get these baits deeper into grass than you can a spinnerbait too."

Making it work

Both Griffin and Gibson like to start the day on top with the soft plastic swimbaits. The Okeechobee veteran typically uses a 1/16-ounce bullet weight that helps part the grass on his topwater retrieves. But in dealing with sparser vegetation on lakes such as Alabama's Eufaula, Gibson often goes weightless.

"Later on in the day, I'll add a ¼-ounce tungsten weight," the tournament angler said. "And as the sun gets higher, I'll go even deeper with a 3/16. What you want to do is follow the fish down with it."

When the bass stop biting in and along the grass, Gibson will back off to the nearest creek channels and ditches. "The fish sometimes move out of the grass with the shad," he explained. "That's when you can use this bait like a crankbait. Just throw it right down the middle. It has a thinner profile and a little different action that most crankbaits, but it will catch fish this way."

If the bass stay in and around the grass, as they often do on Lake Okeechobee, then Griffin, who grew up on the lake, knows best how to catch bass throughout the day on "swimming worms."

Transition areas are among the best locations, he believes. "That's any place the grass changes from one kind to another, such as Kissimmee to needle or finger reed patches."

He also likes grass running onto cattail points, and, of course, edges, which he will fish parallel. "That's when you might want to swim it underneath," Griffin said. "And you might want to give the bait an up and down or in and out erratic movement."

Also be sure to swim your bait across and drop it into pockets, especially if you are fishing during or just before or after the spawn, Griffin advises. "Fish key on those places anytime they're around the spawn mode," he said. "In the beginning it can be difficult to see those little pockets, especially in needle grass."

At Lake Eufaula, Gibson learned that bass like to use these pockets as ambush points. "There's probably going to be a bass sitting under the (grass) mat around that hole, waiting to eat whatever swims by in that little area of open water."

Most important for consistent success, Griffin added, is to watch how bass respond. "If they wake up behind your bait, but won't take it, then you might need to slow down. Sometimes they might want a different profile."

Be prepared

You don't need a stiff rod, braided line, and a heavy wide-gap hook to fish soft plastic swimbaits. But you do if you want to catch fish consistently with them, especially in grass.

Gibson likes a 7-0 heavy action rod, paired with 15- or 30-pound braid. The lighter line is for swimming the bait underwater, the heavier for topwater.

The primary benefit of braid is that it has no stretch, facilitating quicker and more powerful hooksets. Lighter braid, meanwhile, allows for longer casts and permits a bait to get deeper faster.

"Others like 65-pound braid, but I've never lost a fish on 15 and 30 and the lighter braid is cleaner to throw," Gibson said.

For hooks, Gibson, Griffin, and Reynolds all recommend at least a 5/0 wide gap, and the two Florida anglers even suggest 7/0 for the thicker baits. A hook weighted at the bend, Reynolds added, will act as a keel and reduce line twist.

In especially thick grass, small screw-in weights are a good option, since they help keep the bait rigged properly and reduce wear on the head.

Of course, preferred wear and tear on the head and other parts of the bait comes from bass eating it, and the soft plastic swimbait is an offering that draws lots of attention and strikes. For many anglers, though, the ratio of bites to bass boated is not good, even with proper tackle.

To help improve your odds, Griffin advises you allow the fish to pull the bait down before you set the hook on a topwater bite. "You have to discipline yourself to not set the hook too quick," he said. "Let 'em have it a little."

Gibson, meanwhile, recommends you determine your hookset based on the depth of the water you're fishing.

"If it's one to two feet deep, hit that fish right away. It has no place to go with the bait and is going to eat it right away.

"You want to reel as hard as you can and set the hook as hard as you can because that fish is coming at you," he said.

"If you're fishing water that's four to seven feet or deeper, let the fish hit and pull against you before you set the hook. That's because the fish doesn't have to eat the bait as soon as it hits it. It's more likely to suck it in as it goes down."

---

46. Here Comes the Sun

*A*uthor's note: You will live longer, be healthier, and, as a result enjoy more days on the water catching more bass if you protect yourself from skin cancer and dehydration. Here's what you should know:

*   *   *   *   *

Especially following a long, cold winter, nothing feels quite like warm sunshine on bare skin. For a bass angler, enjoying the spring sunshine is as much a part of fishing as spooling on new line.

Preston Clark, a pro angler from Florida, knows and appreciates that feeling. He also recognizes the danger of too much of a good thing: More than 90 percent of skin cancers are caused by sun exposure.

"It really hits home when you see someone you've known forever have to give up something they love (fishing) because of skin cancer," he said. "I have a good friend who's had several spots removed. He's 45, the same age as me, and we're right in the demographic of the guys most likely to see signs of actinic keratosis (AK)."

Considered a "pre-cancer," AK is a visible sign of sun damage caused by years of sun exposure. AKs are small, red, sometimes scaly or rough spots, most often occurring on the face, bald scalp, hands, shoulders, and arms. When caught early, they are easily treated with a variety of methods, including excision, laser therapy, topical creams, and freezing with liquid nitrogen.

Left untreated, they can develop into squamous cell carcinoma (SCC), one of three types of skin cancer. Medical experts say that 40 to 60 percent of squamous cell carcinomas begin as untreated AKs, with 2 to 10 percent of SCCs becoming invasive and life-threatening.

While annual screenings and treatment are important, preventative actions can help keep away the AKs and skin cancer, according to Dr. Neil Fenske, professor and chair of the Department of Dermatology and Cutaneous Surgery at the University of South Florida.

"You don't develop skin cancer because of a one-time shot of sun," he said. "You need multiple hits, which eventually cause DNA damage and genetic changes. The skin goes from normal to abnormal to cancerous."

With enough unprotected exposure, you still can develop AKs and/or cancer even if you don't burn, he added.

The good news is that, given the opportunity, skin can repair itself. "I have patients I've been seeing for 30 years whose skin is better today than it was years ago," Fenske said. "There's still much to be gained by protecting yourself, even when older."

The best way to protect skin is to stay out of the sun, he continued. Next best is clothing, followed by sun blocks and screens. "A tan doesn't protect you from skin cancer," he added. "It's a sign of skin injury."

Tournament anglers know the dangers of too much sun, Clark said, adding that many "cover up" when the cameras aren't around. "But there's still a lot of work to be done to educate people," he said.

Often overlooked

Exhausted after a day on the water? Think you're getting too old or out of condition to maintain the pace? I have good news. Yes, you are getting older, but too old? Probably not. And, yes, exercise is important, especially if you put on a few pounds over the years.

But there's another likely contributor to your exhaustion, one that is often overlooked—dehydration. This is especially true if you're fishing in the southern United States, Mexico, Central, and South America, or any other tropical or subtropical areas. But it can happen anywhere.

Avoid dehydration and you won't be nearly so tired at the end of the day. You'll also avoid skull-splitting headaches that seemingly appear out of nowhere. A good friend and veteran Florida angler says that he tries to consume six to eight ounces of water or sports drinks every half-hour.

"If you wait until you're thirsty to start taking in fluids, it's too late," he warns, adding that moderately cooled drinks of 45 to 55 degrees are absorbed faster into the body than those kept ice cold. "I just squeeze a little lemon or lime in the water and it makes for a very refreshing drink."

He stays away from caffeinated sodas, coffee, and tea, which act as diuretics and actually increase dehydration. He avoids beer and other alcoholic drinks for the same reason.

Unfortunately, too many people avoid even the beneficial fluids. Studies show most people will drink only enough to replace 2/3 of fluids lost.

Up to 80 percent of water is lost through perspiration, as the body, much like a machine, struggles to keep from overheating. Without replacement of that fluid, the cardiovascular system becomes impaired and can't deliver the oxygen and nutrients needed to keep muscles functioning without undue strain. The result: fatigue.

In addition, if fluid is not replaced, the body can't maintain its cooling mechanism, resulting in other symptoms, such as headaches, nausea, and cramps. Prolonged denial of necessary life-giving water can lead to fast heartbeat, low blood pressure, shock, and even death. The American College of Sports Medicine makes these recommendations:

- Drink 16 ounces of fluids about two hours before exposing yourself to heat and/or sun. This gives the body plenty of time to regulate its fluid levels in preparation for perspiration and helps delay or avoid the effects of dehydration.
- Once fishing, drink before becoming thirsty and drink at frequent intervals to replace fluid lost through sweating. Approximately eight ounces of fluid is needed to replace each pound of body weight lost.
- People tend to drink more if the liquid tastes good. Take along plenty of sweetened and/or flavored energy drinks if you like those better than water.

47. What I Learned the Hard Way

*E*ager to fish, I tied on a jig and, with my rod tip hanging over the edge of the boat, I cut the tag end of the line. Or rather I intended to cut the tag end. In my haste, I cut the main line and then watched my new $4 bait sink into the depths.

That's the "uh-oh" moment I remember best. But I've had others, as have all of my angler friends. Cutting the main line instead of the tag ranks right up there as among the most common—and infuriating. So does culling the wrong fish in a tournament.

Why do we do it? Why do we not remember if we brushed our teeth, turned off the lights, or locked the door? Those actions become rote and we stop paying attention. We let body memory take over while our mind is elsewhere.

In bass fishing, not paying attention can cost you a bait, a fish, a tournament win, or even your life.

As I leaned over the side to net a friend's fish, I suddenly found myself underwater with the net in my hand. I can't describe what happened because I don't know. One moment I was in a nice, dry boat and the next I was fighting through icy water to regain the surface on a blustery March day. It was as if there was no in between, no brief moment of panic when I knew I was falling overboard.

After thinking long and hard about that frightening moment, I suspect I went swimming fully clothed because my center of gravity—chest and shoulders—extended over the edge of the boat as I leaned for the fish. And the rest of me followed.

Whatever the reason, I've learned to focus on each and every thing I do while fishing, especially if I'm in a boat. And I've made a conscious effort to learn from my mistakes. That way, when I find myself in situations similar to those that turned out badly in the past, I don't repeat my errors. And, not coincidentally, I believe I catch more fish.

Looking back, my first "uh, oh" moment occurred when I was 11 or 12 and fishing alone for bluegill from the shore of a little lake. Somehow I figured out that cooperative fish were about six feet deep. I quickly put on a fresh worm, moved the bobber the appropriate distance up from the bait, and let fly with a sidearm cast from the left side. As I swept back with the rod, the line whipped around the right side of my face and the hook stuck in the lower lid of my right eye, worm and all.

So there I was, fishing alone, with a hook embedded in my face and about a mile from home. But that wasn't the worst of it. That wasn't the "uh, oh" moment. That was just a kid's carelessness and, as it turned out, the injury was superficial. The "uh, oh" moment came when I realized I had no pocket knife to cut the line hanging from the hook. No way could I hold the rod in one hand, with line draped all over the place, and ride my bike home. Fortunately, a kind stranger in a pickup did have a pocket knife. He snipped the line and took me to a hospital emergency room.

In the decades since, I've always carried a knife with me when I go fishing. And I never again made a sidearm cast with six feet of line hanging below a bobber.

Here's what else I've learned the hard way, most all of it related to one word of advice: Focus.

1. Be sensitive.

Most any rod will land a fish once you have it hooked. But you need a sensitive rod to feel many of the bites. And as you're working that bait, especially on the bottom, you must pay attention. Many anglers miss bites and bass for those two reasons, and they don't even realize they have missed them.

2. Slow is smooth. Smooth is fast.

Don't be distracted by thoughts of making the first cast or catching a fish before your partner does. That's exactly what slows you down, as you fumble to thread line through the eyes of your rod or tie on a bait—and sometimes forget to make certain your drag is set properly.

3. Don't blame the bass.

Fish don't break line. Anglers do, usually because they pull too hard or have the drag set too tight. Sometimes it's because they neglected to check for frays for too long a time.

4. Food and fluids.

You can much more clearly concentrate on fishing when you're not hungry or thirsty. Some people mistakenly believe they don't have time to eat or drink. Actually, if you want to perform at your best level, you do need food and fluids. That's just as important as fishing in the right place or choosing the most effective bait.

Dehydration can sneak up on you, especially if you're fishing in full sun. It will slow you down, muddle your thoughts, and, if bad enough, give you a throbbing headache before you ever realize you're thirsty.

That's just what happened to me one February day while fishing phosphate pits in Florida. The temperature was no more than 70 or so, but sun was bright and I neglected to drink water as I eagerly cast for bass. The headache pain was suddenly so debilitating that I had to stop fishing. Fortunately, drinking two liters of water eased and eventually eliminated the discomfort, but I didn't feel normal for the rest of the day.

Consume fluids *before* you get thirsty.

5. Heed nature's call.

If you have to relieve yourself, do it! Make your first priority finding a private place to let 'er rip. Otherwise, angry bowels or a bloated bladder will override your focus on trying to catch fish.

And on a related note, generally it's a good idea to avoid rich meals late at night before you go fishing early the next day.

---

48. School Is Out; Here's Your Homework

*O*kay, boys and girls, that's it for today. It's time for you to go fishing. Of course, I do have some homework for you.

Oh, Clarence, stop whining. This is for your own good. Doing what I've outlined for you here will help you kick some bass. I don't expect perfection. We all make mistakes from time to time. But if you make an honest effort to do all of these things as a matter of habit, you will be a better angler.

1. Think of your rods, reels, lines, and baits as power tools.

Keep them in good working order and they will perform well for you. Just as importantly, make sure to choose the right tools for the job at hand.

2. Practice casting.

Possibly more than anything else, what separates the pros from the rest of us is their casting accuracy. Putting your bait exactly where you want it on the first try saves time and effort and increases the likelihood that you're going to catch a bass—if it's there.

Don't have the time to spend on the water that the pros do? Put a tire or other target in your backyard and practice there.

3. Be observant.

Wind, weather, water conditions, and feeding activity by both fish and birds will help you figure out what's going on if you pay attention. Also, take note of what your partner is doing down to most minute detail, if he's catching more and/or bigger fish than you. Don't rely on him to tell you what he's doing. I'm not suggesting he might not be honest with you. I'm saying he may not even be aware of what he's doing differently than you.

4. Know conditions before you go so you can plan accordingly.

What's the barometric pressure doing? What's the forecast? What's happening with the water level? All these factors and more can affect the bite for better or worse, and being aware of conditions can help you plan your strategy for the day.

5. Tie knots carefully and conscientiously.

Of all the guides and pros I've fished with over the years. the majority prefer the Palomar knot. A few use the improved clinch, but they are few and far between. Personally, I still have painful memories of my youth when I lost fish because of poorly tied clinch knots that slipped. Use the one you have most confidence in, but focus on tying it properly and snug it down tightly.

A Palomar works well on all kinds of lines. But if you're using braid, wet the line just a bit before you pull the knot tight. The same goes for fluorocarbon.

Whatever knot you prefer, a drop of glue will help secure it.

6. Check your line frequently for frays and abrasions. It is the weakest line between you and the fish.

Be especially mindful if you're catching lots of bass and/or throwing crankbaits in and around rocks. If you use monofilament or copolymer line and catch lots of quality fish, retie frequently as a matter of habit.

At home, occasionally run a cotton ball through the eyes of your rods. If fiber adheres to metal, you know a rough spot had developed there.

7. Plan to experience occasional backlashes with baitcasting reels. It happens to everyone who uses them.

That's one of the best reasons to take multiple outfits with you. Some backlashes you just can't pick out, at least in a timely manner.

Also, carry a comb. It's great for picking out tangles, especially those your sausage-like fingers just can't reach. For best results, make sure the comb has small, exposed teeth at the end.

8. And speaking of backlashes . . .

I've caught several bass while picking out backlashes, including my largest smallmouth, a 6-pounder. The message here is that we're more likely to fish too fast than too slow.

9. Rig plastics properly.

If you don't, you'll miss bass when you set the hook.

"Properly" means not only pushing the hook through the bait and then skin-hooking the point. It means using an adequate hook for the size and thickness of the bait. Too often fishermen use hooks that are too small. Too often they use straight shank, when they should use wide gap.

Also, the bait should be straight on the hook so it moves properly in the water. To ensure that, stick the hook through the head and then lay the shank alongside the bait. That will show you where to put the hook through the body of the plastic.

10. Keep your hooks sharp.

In general, today's hooks come out of the package much sharper than those in decades past. But that doesn't mean they remain that way. The slightest bend in that razor-sharp point can result in a lost fish.

11. Be flexible.

If the bass aren't biting, don't stubbornly stick with a bait just because it caught fish in the past. You might have to go with a different type, or the fix could be as simple as downsizing. Experiment.

The same goes for location. The most important thing bass tournaments have taught us is that bass are always biting somewhere. You just have to find them.

The real challenge is knowing when to go and when to stay and experiment. Good luck with that.

12. Be irritating.

When bass aren't actively feeding, they often have to be provoked. That means you must discover what triggers their predatory instinct. Often it's a fast-moving bait thrown repeatedly in front of them. Other times . . . who knows?

13. Improve your odds.

You want to catch a big bass? Fish for them when they likely are the heaviest. That's prespawn, with late fall next best.

Also, target fisheries that have a reputation for producing big bass.

14. Get comfortable.

It's not all about the fish and how to catch them. It's also about you fishing at peak efficiency. That means taking care of yourself when you're on the water. Rain gear, cap, sun glasses, sun block, snacks, and beverages are necessities, not luxuries.

15. Enjoy yourself.

In bass fishing, as in most everything else in life, attitude is everything. Act as if you're having a good time, and you will. Think positively about kickin' some bass, and you will.

---

49. About the Author

A long-time senior writer for B.A.S.S. Publications, Robert U. Montgomery has been hooked since he first went fishing on a Cub Scout outing. His degree in journalism from the University of Missouri helped him turn his passion into a career as a fishing writer.

He's fished for bass with the best anglers, guides, and pros across the U.S., as well as in Canada and Mexico; and, in doing so, collected a wealth of insider information he shares with readers in *Kickin' Bass*. Robert also reveals what he learned from his own decades of angling experience, including catching and releasing more than a dozen 10-pound largemouth bass.

The founder of *Activist Angler* website, Montgomery is the author of two other fishing books: *Better Bass Fishing* and *Why We*

Fish. He has also written about nature, rescue dogs, and nostalgia in *Fish, Frogs, and Fireflies, Pippa's Journey*, and *Under the Bed*.

The Missouri native is winner of the prestigious Homer Circle Fishing Communicator Award. He lives on a small lake in the eastern Ozarks with his dog Pippa.

---

50. Quick Tips for Bass Fishing

Choosing a Guide

Questions you should ask:

- Is the guide licensed as required by the state?
- Does he have liability insurance?
- What is the guide's safety record and medical training?
- How many years in business? Some younger guide services can have better customer service and put in more time on the water, attempting to establish a clientele. Yet there is something to be said for longevity, since poor operations go out of business quickly.
- Do you, the angler, need a license and where do you get it?
- What kind of tackle and gear should you bring and what is provided? This includes clothing, food, and drinks. As with the license, this information should be provided on check lists.
- What kind of fishing does the guide anticipate? The best guides make certain their clients understand the options beforehand. And they do their best to accommodate.

- What happens if the weather doesn't cooperate? Make sure you know Plan B, and maybe even Plan C.
- Are you going to be charged for extras?
- Alcohol or no alcohol?

— From Chapter 5, How to Choose a Fishing Guide

Treating Barotrauma in Bass

Barotrauma is injury to the lungs caused by changes in air pressure. For bass, being yanked from the depths of a lake, hauled to the surface, and placed in a holding tank can lead to this condition. Bass give clear signs they're suffering, and you need to act quickly to ensure their welfare. A fish on its side or upside down at the water's surface each time you open the livewell needs treatment. And it needs relief now, not at the weigh-in hours later. Damage to internal organs starts can start the minute you lift the fish from the water.

Fizzing, or relieving barotrauma, is an easily mastered technique. To deflate the swim bladder, use a small gauge hypodermic needle, equipped with a reamer (to keep tissue from plugging the needle), to pierce the skin of the fish at predetermined points on the side, depending on the species of fish. This releases excess gases and returns the fish to neutral buoyancy. *Bassmaster.com* and other websites can show you where to place the needle and provide more detailed instruction.

Neutral buoyancy is the point at which the fish neither sinks nor floats. This is the most important part of the technique to learn, and can only be determined while the fish is in the water. You do not release gas for a certain amount of time, nor do you count to three or five or whatever. You withdraw the needle at the point the fish no longer sinks or floats.

— From Chapter 31, Taking Care of Fizzness

Topwater Wisdom from a Legendary Lure Maker

- Topwater doesn't have to be early (or late). That's just when people used to fish because they worked during the day. Ten to two can be the best time for big fish.
- You can catch bass consistently in water that's 50 degrees or above. In colder water you usually want to fish faster or slower, not in between.
- The popper is a good choice for cold water because you can keep it in one place longer and its tail sits down in the water, making it easier for the fish to take.
- A popper is also the best bait when fish are holding tight to cover. You don't necessarily have to pop it. Just twitch it and let it sit there.
- A bass can suck the bait in like a vacuum cleaner or hit it so hard it knocks the paint off.
- Your reaction time is faster than you think, so be careful. You have to let the fish eat the bait.
- Don't set the hook hard. Just "snug" the bass. It turns sideways after it strikes.
- I use at least 15-pound line. Lighter than that goes limp and gets tangled on the hooks.
- For 85 to 90 percent of my retrieves I use the same cadence, two jerks and let it sit. I let the fish dictate how hard to jerk.
- You want to use a faster retrieve in rough water to take the slack out of the line.
- A bass will hit sometimes just to kill the bait. That's the predator part of the brain. It's being mean, just like a junk yard dog. You want to "feel" the fish before you set the hook.
- Eighty five percent of my bites come when the bait is still or coming to a stop.
- The size of the lure is more important than the color.

- I use black and white (topwater baits) 75 percent of the time. And, personally, I think a little red under the nose and tail helps. Most of those color choices are just a "between the ears" thing. Usually, it's the action, not the color.
- Mylar tinsel on the back hook gets me 25 percent more bites. Glitter on the sides (of bait) gets their attention from farther away.
- The same bait will catch fish anywhere. It's a matter of confidence. That's why there are regional favorites.
- Throw to anything different, like where two different types of grasses meet. Where pepper grass meets bulrushes is the best. Also, throw in the holes.

— From Chapter 39, Top Secrets

Hookset Advice from Kevin VanDam

You'll catch more bass if you set the hook properly. Here's how Kevin VanDam says you should do it.

Texas-rig soft plastics: Drive the hook through the plastic. "I like a little slack line. I drop the rod tip and hit real hard," he says.

Spinnerbaits: Use more of a pull set. Let the rod load up and pull into the fish. Reel hard and pull.

Topwaters: Reel until you feel the weight of the fish and then set the hook. You don't need to set the hook hard.

Crankbaits: Reel and pull.

Light-tackle spinning gear: Don't jerk at all. Reel set. Reel fast and let the rod load up before you pull.

Braided line: Don't need to jerk nearly as hard. That's important to remember because there's no give there, as with monofilament.

— From Chapter 42, Hookset Advice from KVD

Avoiding Dehydration

- Drink 16 ounces of fluids about two hours before exposing yourself to heat and/or sun. This gives the body plenty of time to regulate its fluid levels in preparation for perspiration and helps delay or avoid the effects of dehydration.
- Once fishing, drink before becoming thirsty and drink at frequent intervals to replace fluid lost through sweating. Approximately eight ounces of fluid is needed to replace each pound of body weight lost.
- People tend to drink more if the liquid tastes good. Take along plenty of sweetened and/or flavored energy drinks if you like those better than water.

— *From Chapter 46, Here Comes the Sun*

Top Ten Tips for Being a Better Angler

1. Think of your rods, reels, lines, and baits as power tools.

Keep them in good working order and they will perform well for you. Make sure to choose the right tools for the job at hand.

2. Practice casting.

Possibly more than anything else, what separates the pros from the rest of us is their casting accuracy. Don't have the time to spend on the water that the pros do? Put a tire or other target in your backyard and practice there.

3. Be observant.

Wind, weather, water conditions, and feeding activity by both fish and birds will help you figure out what's going on if you pay attention. Also, take note of what your partner is doing down to most minute detail, if he's catching more and/or bigger fish than you. Don't rely on him to tell you what he's doing. He may not even be aware of what he's doing differently than you.

4. Know conditions before you go so you can plan accordingly.

What's the barometric pressure doing? What's the forecast? What's happening with the water level? All these factors and more can affect the bite for better or worse, and being aware of conditions can help you plan your strategy for the day.

5. Tie knots carefully and conscientiously.

Of all the guides and pros I've fished with over the years. the majority prefer the Palomar knot. A few use the improved clinch, but they are few and far between.

A Palomar works well on all kinds of lines. But if you're using braid, wet the line just a bit before you pull the knot tight. The same goes for fluorocarbon.

6. Check your line frequently for frays and abrasions. It is the weakest line between you and the fish.

7. Slow Down

I've caught several bass while picking out backlashes, including my largest smallmouth, a 6-pounder. The message here is that we're more likely to fish too fast than too slow.

8. Rig plastics properly.

If you don't, you'll miss bass when you set the hook.

"Properly" means not only pushing the hook through the bait and then skin-hooking the point. It means using an adequate hook for the size and thickness of the bait.

Also, the bait should be straight on the hook so it moves properly in the water.

9. Keep your hooks sharp.

In general, today's hooks come out of the package much sharper than those in decades past. But that doesn't mean they remain that way. The slightest bend in that razor-sharp point can result in a lost fish.

10. Be flexible.

If the bass aren't biting, don't stubbornly stick with a bait just because it caught fish in the past. You might have to go with a different type, or the fix could be as simple as downsizing. Experiment.

The same goes for location. The most important thing bass tournaments have taught us is that bass are always biting somewhere. You just have to find them.

— *From Chapter 48, School Is Out; Here's Your Homework*

Made in the USA
Las Vegas, NV
15 September 2021